ESSAYS ON ROBERTSONIAN ECONOMICS

ESSAYS ON ROBERTSONIAN ECONOMICS

Edited by

John R. Presley
Professor of Economics
Loughborough University

St. Martin's Press

© John R. Presley 1992

First published in Great Britain 1992 by
THE MACMILLAN PRESS LTD
Houndmills, Basingstoke, Hampshire RG21 2XS
and London
Companies and representatives
throughout the world

A catalogue record for this book is available
from the British Library

ISBN 0–333–55880–4

Printed in Great Britain by
Antony Rowe, Chippenham, Wiltshire

First published in the United States of America 1992 by
Scholarly and Reference Division,
ST. MARTIN'S PRESS, INC.,
175 Fifth Avenue,
New York, N.Y. 10010

ISBN 0–312–06826–3

Library of Congress Cataloging-in-Publication Data
Essays on Robertsonian economics / edited by John R. Presley.
p.   cm.
Includes index.
ISBN 0–312–06826–3
1. Robertson, Dennis Holme, Sir, 1890–1963.   2. Business cycles.
3. Money.   I. Presley, John R.
HB103.R62E87   1992
338.5'42—dc20   91–38713
                                                     CIP

Contents

List of Text Illustrations

Acknowledgements

I am grateful to those who originally published some of the articles contained in this volume, and have permitted them to be reproduced, sometimes in adapted form: the first chapter is adapted from Chapter 1 of *Robertsonian Economics* (London: Macmillan; New York: Holmes and Meier, 1979); the second chapter was first published as Discussion Paper no. 92 by the Financial Marketing Group of the London School of Economics and Political Science; the third chapter is adapted from an article in the *Journal of Economic Literature*, 18, 1980; the fourth chapter first appeared in the *Federal Reserve Bank of Richmond Economic Review* in 1980; the fifth chapter first appeared in *Research in the History of Economics and Methodology*, 6, 1989; the sixth chapter first appeared in the *Economic Journal*, 1953; and the last chapter in the *American Economic Review*, 42 (3), 1952.

The utmost gratitude must go, of course, to the various contributors – Professor Thomas Wilson, Professor Charles Goodhart, Professor Thomas Humphrey and the late Professor William Fellner. One other person, in particular, has been very influential and of great assistance in putting this volume together and I owe him special thanks. This is Professor Stanley Dennison, formerly Vice-Chancellor of Hull University and pupil, friend and colleague of Sir Dennis Holme Robertson. I will forever be in his debt for his continuous support for my research on Robertsonian economics over a twenty-year period.

I would also like to express my thanks to the ESRC, to the British Academy and also the Wincott Foundation, who at various times have provided financial assistance for my research on Robertsonian Economics.

Finally, I wish to express my thanks to Mrs Joyce Tuson who has, with her usual efficiency, typed this manuscript. My gratitude goes also to my wife, Barbara, and to Mrs Jean Smith who have prepared the index.

JOHN R. PRESLEY

Preface

As Professor Presley points out in Chapter One, throughout the almost thirty years since Sir Dennis Robertson died, his outstanding contributions to the understanding of economic phenomena have been largely neglected. Without going into detail, two examples might be given. First, a popular dictionary of economics published in 1972, with frequent reprints and new editions in 1978 and 1984, again with reprints, has no entry for Robertson or any reference to his work, against a long entry for Keynes and also substantial ones for two of his followers (Joan Robinson and Kaldor). There is also an entry for A.W.H. Phillips, with a largely uncritical exposition of the 'Phillips curve' as a guide to policy. Secondly, in most British universities few students read a word of Robertson or are informed by their teachers of his contributions, which in turn reflects their own limitations. Instead they are mostly fed on the latest dogmas of debased neo-Keynesianism and mathematical growth models.

The relegation of Robertson to the scrap-heap was much less marked in the United States and Europe, where interest in and knowledge of his work continued. At the outset, there had been some highly critical reviews of Keynes' *General Theory* and critical comment continued, while in spite of the efforts of various popularisers, the basic doctrines never became, as they did in Britain, the accepted orthodoxy which Robertson predicted would be even more dogmatic than that of the system against which it was supposed to be a revolution – as indeed is what happens in so many revolutions. Equally, the influence on policy of neo-Keynesianism was never so marked as it was in Britain. Moreover, far from a growing unanimity of ideas and opinions which Keynes in the 1920s hoped for and even predicted, there has been increasing divergence on almost every aspect. An outstanding case is the present disarray on almost everything related to inflation – its desirability (or undesirability), its causes, its effects (especially on employment and 'growth') and appropriate policies.

This was, of course, one of Robertson's main concerns throughout his life's work, from the *Study of Industrial Fluctuation* (1915) to his evidence for the Canadian Royal Commission (1963), the intervening Reports of the Cohen Council (which he drafted) in 1958 and 1959, and the various papers written after he retired from his Professorship between 1956 and 1963 which have now (1992) been published for the first time in *Robertson and Economic Policy* to celebrate his centenary. These are vastly superior to most of what has been written in the past twenty years. He consistently regarded stability of the general price level as a primary objective, but with flexibility of individual prices according to changes in demands, in productivity in different industries, in international trading relationships and many other factors. This is something which is now largely neglected, with the simplistic aggregates of some' macro-economists paying no regard to micro analysis, even applying macro concepts to situations which cry out for micro treatment (a good example is advocates of minimum wages stating that they cannot cause unemployment because the higher wages are incomes which will be spent in purchasing the products of the industry and hence *increasing* the demand for labour).

It is to be hoped that at least some economists of the present generation will read these six essays and realise that there is a major contribution which Robertson made and can still make not only to the understanding of basic principles but also of contemporary problems. The essays have been chosen to represent the various facets of his work, though the emphasis is on industrial fluctuation and monetary problems. It is also significant that two are from the United States, and particular attention should be paid to Fellner's essay on the *Robertsonian Evolution*.

It might also even be hoped that some will read Robertson's work for themselves. He used to comment that much of the study of the history of economic ideas (which was once part of virtually every university course) was based on books about other books, often third- rather than second-hand, and that it was essential to study the original writings. He was himself steeped in them; in the long vacation of 1910 before he changed from classics to economics, he read *The Wealth of Nations* and Marshall's *Principles*, making a summary of the latter, and continued to refresh his understanding whenever necessary; his copy of Marshall contains many marginalia referring to later work (e.g. that of Hicks) as he studied it. He was well-versed in other great classical economists, as well as in economic history, especially of the eighteenth and nineteenth centuries, in both of which respects many of the later generations of Cambridge economists, and especially his critics, were sadly deficient.

The rewards of reading Robertson are great. Much can be learned not only in greater understanding of economic processes and deeper knowledge but also in what used to be called methodology. An outstanding feature of his work, learned largely from Adam Smith and Alfred Marshall, is the blend of rigorous analysis with profound study of relevant data with, in Marshall's terms, a ceaseless search for new inductions to supplement and correct deductive analysis. In this he had few equals, and they did not include Keynes who, in spite of his extensive knowledge, could in his more mercurial moods make sweeping generalisations, historical and statistical, based on little more than his own fertile imagination.

The Robertsonian world is entirely different from that of the abstract, often mathematical, models which are used to lay down policy without regard to the particular circumstances of the matters at issue. Thus we have his insistence that not every trade cycle has the same characteristics, that in particular the Great Depression of the late 1920s and early 1930s, which dominated Keynesianism, was in many ways unique, and that it was impossible to prescribe neat packets of therapeutic pills which could be universally applied. Another case is that of the proliferation of models of 'growth', which he ridiculed in his Marshall lectures, and which have done so much to obfuscate the real problems of under-developed countries and to intensify their poverty.

Another feature related to this is his emphasis on the limitations of economics and economists in determining policies. This again has two aspects. One is that economic factors are far from being the whole of life or any problem, that in determining policy regard must be paid to other elements in which the economist has no special expertise. The other is that on occasion the economic elements are subject to intense disagreement. The result is that the economist should exercise restraint and even humility in his advocacy of policies. Again this is in marked contrast to the arrogant certainty of so many neo-Keynesians, and salutary advice at a time when many who are ill-qualified to do so pronounce and pontificate on every issue as soon as it arises, often in advance by predicting, usually wrongly, what will happen.

Last, but by no means least, reading Robertson is a constant delight. His mastery of language is complete, and his prose is absolutely precise and unambiguous, with never a surplus word: he once said that it would be better if economic discussion was conducted in Latin rather than English, or even more German. On occasion he would invent a word if there was no other way of expressing his meaning – a good example is 'ecfare'. There is also frequent use of illuminating metaphor and much felicitous humour, as in the quotations from the *Alice* books. This should not be allowed to obscure his deadly seriousness or enormous integrity as a scholar. Indeed, it is often used as a device to emphasize the significance of what he is conveying: who but he could have written *A Non-Econometrician's Lament*?

Professor Presley's work is highly commended as a notable contribution to restoring Robertson to his rightful place in the development of economics and its relevance to the progress of opulence.

S. R. DENNISON

Notes on the Contributors

S. R. Dennison was a pupil of D. H. Robertson at Trinity College, Cambridge 1933–35, and also a member of Keynes's private Political Economy Club. He was then a Lecturer at Manchester University, maintaining close contact with Robertson. During the war they were both working in London and met regularly. From 1946 to 1958, they were together at Cambridge, with Dennison holding a university lectureship, and closely collaborating on many matters, continuing after Robertson retired from the professorship in 1957, and finally acting as his executor. Subsequent appointments were Professor at the Queen's University of Belfast and the University of Newcastle upon Tyne and Vice-Chancellor of the University of Hull, from which he retired in 1979.

William Fellner was born in Budapest in 1905; he studied at the University of Budapest, the Federal Institute of Technology in Zurich and at Berlin University, where he received a doctorate in 1929. He was a partner in a family manufacturing company between 1929–38; in 1938 he went to the USA, joining the economics faculty at the University of California at Berkeley in 1939; by 1947 he was a full professor; in 1952 he became Professor of Economics at Yale University and in 1959 he moved to the Sterling Professorship at the same university, retiring in 1973. He was president of the American Economics Association in 1969. Amongst his numerous books, the better known are *Competition Among the Few* (1949), *Towards a Reconstruction of Macroeconomics* (1976) and *Monetary Policies and Full Employment* (1946).

Charles Goodhart was born in 1936 in London. He went up to Trinity College, Cambridge for his university education in 1957. Goodhart took a PhD at Harvard before returning to Trinity as a Prize Fellow. He worked in the Department of Economic Affairs, and at the London School of Economics (LSE), for a few years, before becoming adviser on domestic monetary policy at the Bank of England, 1968–85. He then returned to academic life at LSE as Norman Sosnow Professor of Banking and Finance. He is the author of several books on monetary history, including *The Evolution of Central Banks*, a monetary textbook, *Money, Information and Uncertainty*, and numerous articles on monetary history, financial institutions, the foreign exchange market, and monetary policy, a small selection of which were collected in *Monetary Theory and Practice*.

Thomas M. Humphrey was born in Louisville, Kentucky in 1935 and completed his education at the University of Tennessee (BSc 1958, MSc 1960) and Tulane University (PhD, 1970). He taught economics at American schools in the South including Auburn University, University of Georgia, Mary Washington University, St Andrews Presbyterian College, Tulane University, University of Virginia, Virginia Commonwealth University, and Wofford College. Since 1970 he has been an economist with the Federal Reserve Bank of Richmond where he edits and writes for the Bank's *Economic Review*. He is the author of *Essays on Inflation* (5th edition, 1986), *From Trade-Offs to Policy Ineffectiveness : A History of the Phillips Curve* (1986), *The Monetary Approach to the Balance of Payments, Exchange Rates, and World Inflation* (co-author R. Keleher, 1982) and of numerous journal articles on monetary and banking theory and the history of economic thought.

John Presley was born in 1945; he was educated at Lancaster University (BA), and Loughborough University (PhD). In 1969 he was appointed Lecturer at Loughborough University; in 1976 he became Senior Lecturer; in 1981 Reader in Economics and in 1984 he was appointed Professor of Economics. Between 1985–9 he was the founding Director of the Banking Centre at Loughborough University. Other appointments have included Senior Economic Adviser, Ministry of Planning, Saudi Arabia (1978–9), visiting scholar, Harvard University (1982) and visiting Professorial Fellow, Nottingham University (1989–90). He has written several books on monetary policy, the economics of the Middle East and the history of economic thought. These include *Robertsonian Economics* (1978), and *Pioneers of Modern Economics* (joint editor/contributor, two volumes 1981, 1989), *European Monetary Integration* (1971), *Currency Areas* (1976) (with G. E. J. Dennis), *The Saudia Arabian Economy* (1981, 1989) (with A. J. Westaway) and *Banking in the Arab Gulf* (1991) (with R. Wilson).

Thomas Wilson was born in Northern Ireland in 1916 and took his first degree at the Queen's University, Belfast, in 1938. He then went to LSE and obtained a London University doctorate in 1940. He worked for a time in the Ministry of Economic Warfare and then in the Ministry of Aircraft Production before being transferred to the Prime Minister's Statistical Branch. After the war, he was elected to a Fellowship at University College, Oxford, and also became editor of the Oxford Economics Papers. In 1958, he was appointed to the Adam Smith Chair of Political Economy at the University of Glasgow, where he remained until his retirement in 1982. He is a Fellow of the British Academy, a Fellow of the Royal Society of Edinburgh and an Honorary Fellow of the London School of Economics. His books include: *Fluctuations in Income and Employment*, (1942); *Modern Capitalism and Economic Progress* (1950); *Oxford Studies in the Price Mechanism*, joint editor with P. W. S. Andrews (1951); *Inflation* (1951); *Planning and Growth* (1964); two books to mark the bicentenary of *The Wealth of Nations* (1976) – *Essays on Adam Smith*, and *The Market and the State*, contributor and joint editor with A. S. Skinner; *The Political Economy of the Welfare State*, with D. J. Wilson (1982); *Inflation, Unemployment and the Market* (1984); *Ulster – Conflict and Consent (1989)*; *The State and Social Welfare*, contributor and joint editor with D. J. Wilson (1991).

1 Introduction

This volume is not intended as a full biography of Sir Dennis Holme Robertson.[1] Its focus is upon the most important aspects of his work as an economist – his theory of industrial fluctuation, his contribution to the development of monetary economics, his views on economic policy and his collaboration with John Maynard Keynes.

It is now twenty-seven years since Robertson died; in 1990 the centenary of his birth was celebrated, yet throughout this period his contribution to economics, with few exceptions,[2] has been neglected. This is despite the fact that much of modern economics can be seen in Robertson's early work. This book, with its sister volume, *Robertson on Economic Policy*,[3] is an attempt to put this right and to serve as a centenary appreciation of Robertsonian Economics.

SIR DENNIS HOLME ROBERTSON – IN AND OUT OF CAMBRIDGE

It is now seventy-five years since Robertson's first book was published.[4] This contained the skeleton of his theory of industrial fluctuation, a theory which he held throughout his lifetime, and which was suitably covered with flesh in the multitude of publications which followed until his death in 1963.

He was born in 1890, the youngest of six children and the son of the Headmaster of Haileybury School. The Robertsons originated from Scotland and had for generations been principally clergymen or schoolmasters. In the year Dennis Robertson was born, his father resigned from his post at Haileybury and became a country parson at Whittlesford in Cambridgeshire. In many ways Dennis Robertson benefitted from this move, for his father was able to devote himself to his children's education. In 1902, already well educated in the classics, he went to Eton; here he excelled, making many friends and becoming captain of the school.[5]

From Eton he gained a classical scholarship to Trinity College, Cambridge in 1908. He continued to prosper both academically and socially, gaining a I-i in the first part of the classical tripos in 1910 whilst enjoying himself thoroughly in Cambridge. He took an active part in amateur dramatics and continued to develop his musical interests.[6] He won, in three successive years, the Chancellor's Prize for English Verse.

Fortunately for the economics profession he was not to stay a classical scholar. In 1910 he turned to the economics tripos gaining a first in Part II of the tripos in 1912; this was achieved despite his many and varied non-academic interests in Cambridge, amongst which were numbered his activities as President of both the Liberal Society and the Union.

Cambridge economics and Marshallian economics were synonymous at that time. Although Robertson was not taught by Marshall, who had retired in 1908, the *Principles of Economics* remained the recommended textbook. A. C. Pigou and J. M. Keynes, both former pupils of Marshall, continued to uphold the Marshallian tradition during Robertson's undergraduate studies. It was J. M. Keynes who became Robertson's Director of Studies; this was the beginning of a very long and productive partnership which flourished especially in the 1920s, but which was to suffer as a result of the 'Keynesian Revolution' in the late 1930s.[7]

After graduation Robertson remained as a research student in Cambridge. In 1914 his research thesis won him a Trinity Fellowship (in the previous year the thesis had gained the Cobden Prize); it also became his first book in 1915. But the war interrupted his academic work; he joined the army and after service in England he was posted to Egypt and Palestine.[8] He did not return to the Trinity Fellowship until 1919.

This heralded the beginning of his most productive period as a monetary economist. His most widely read book, *Money*, was published in 1922 as a Cambridge Economic Handbook. This was a textbook for undergraduates, but it quickly established Robertson's reputation as a monetary expert. It remained in the forefront as a textbook on monetary theory until the 1950s and appeared in a new edition as late as 1948. M. Friedman has seen fit to remark that it 'is a masterpiece of exposition as well as of content'.[9] But *Money* was only the first of a number of writings in the inter-war period which attempted to analyse the role of monetary factors in the trade cycle. *A Study of Industrial Fluctuation* (hereafter referred to as the *Study*) had presented a *real* theory of industrial fluctuation. It was a purpose of later writings to examine the behaviour of money, the rate of interest, and saving and investment in the cycle, and from this to establish the most appropriate types of counter-cyclical policies. In Chapter Three below, Professor Tom Wilson examines Robertson's contribution to the development of monetary theory.

The collaboration between Keynes and Robertson in the 1920s resulted in several major works, though none were published under joint authorship. These works included not only *Money*, but also the *Tract on Monetary Reform*,[10] *Banking Policy and the Price Level* (hereafter referred to as *Banking*) and the *Treatise on Money*.[11] The 1930s witnessed less of a combined effort. Each went their separate ways, Robertson developing the theory of fluctuation he had expounded in 1915, whilst Keynes worked on *The General Theory of Employment, Interest and Money* (hereafter referred to as the *General Theory*). After 1936 they became involved in a debate over the validity of Keynes's theory. This partnership was significant in the development of both Robertsonian and Keynesian economics; for this reason Chapter Five explores their relationship in the inter-war period in more detail.[12]

Robertson also continued to be actively interested in liberal policy, again to some extent working alongside J. M. Keynes. He had been brought up in a Cambridge which had little respect for state controls, but which did tolerate some interference with the free enterprise economy.[13] He was not a socialist; he, for example, regarded Cole's suggestion for the establishment of co-operatives as belonging to the realm of 'Cloud-Cuckoo Land'.[14] Yet at the same time he was not a staunch defender of capitalism. In fact in Mr Ernest Benn's fourfold classification of economists according to their degree of support for capitalism, Robertson remarked, 'I knew that I should come out, if not in the lowest class yet not very far away'.[15] Robertson never had serious political ambitions; his involvement went as far as contributing to Liberal Party Summer Schools, and to policy documents, but no further.

With the exception of eight months spent travelling in the Far East in 1926–7, and four months spent in India (1933–4) working on a statistical enquiry with A. L. Bowley, Robertson remained in Cambridge until 1938. Then he was invited to become a member of the Appointment

Board for the Chair in Banking at the London School of Economics. He declined this invitation, preferring instead to be considered as a candidate for the post. He was duly elected to the Chair and so was able to escape from the ferment of the Keynesian revolution taking place in Cambridge at that time. He taught at the London School of Economics for one year only before the outbreak of the Second World War.

During the war he worked as an economic adviser to Sir F. Phillips who was the Third Secretary in the Treasury with particular responsibility for overseas finance. This work took Robertson to Washington in 1943, where he assisted in the preparations for the Bretton Woods Conference. Here again he was to work with Keynes as a member of the British delegation. On Pigou's retirement he was able to return to Cambridge as Professor of Economics. He occupied this post until his retirement in 1957.[16] Much of his energy was devoted in this post-war period to his lectures in Cambridge (which were published in three volumes),[17] and to general policy issues. After Keynes's death, he did not apply the same vigour to the theoretical debate surrounding the Keynesian revolution, but he still remained its strongest critic.

He gave evidence to the Macmillan Committee on Finance and Industry in May 1930,[18] and to the Canadian Royal Commission on Banking and Finance in 1962.[19] He was a leading member of the Royal Commission on Equal Pay (1944–6), and the only economist amongst the 'three wise men' of the Cohen Council on Prices, Productivity and Incomes (1957–8). Honorary degrees were given to him by several British universities as well as those he received with great pride from Louvain, Columbia, Amsterdam and Harvard. He became a Fellow of the British Academy in 1932, and was knighted in 1953.

He wrote nine books covering almost every aspect of economics,[20] and had ninety-one articles published between September 1912 and September 1962, of which no fewer than thirty appeared in the *Economic Journal*. Many articles were collected to form six further books over the period 1931–66.[21]

WHY STUDY ROBERTSON'S WORK?

From this brief biography one can begin to ascertain the importance of

Robertson in the development of economics; his work is of crucial importance to economists and economic policy makers for two main reasons:

(i) His publications provide a *major* contribution to the study of cyclical movements in the economy. This is highlighted in Chapter Two below by Professor Charles Goodhart's examination of Robertson's work on the real business cycle, and in Professor Wilson's chapter on Effective Demand and the Trade Cycle. Commenting upon the subject matter of fluctuations, money, credit and employment, Robertson himself states: 'this has always been to me the most interesting part of economics – the only part to which I can hope to be remembered as having made any personal contribution'.[22] The importance of this contribution has to some extent already been appreciated by economists. Fellner writes in Chapter Seven:

> after so many years a surprisingly small part of Robertson's early contribution is outmoded in the sense that a problem with which it is concerned seems to have lost the significance, or in the sense that a statement is clearly less adequate than later statements of other authors on the same subject.[23]

One purpose of this book is to show that this statement is still valid in 1992.

(ii) We have already seen that Robertson worked with, and was influenced by J. M. Keynes in the inter-war period. Referring to the development of Keynes's work Lord Robbins argues: 'no-one with even a speck of justice in his make-up could deny to Sir Dennis a very appreciable share of the credit'.[24] The publication of the *Collected Writings of John Maynard Keynes*[25] not only enables a closer examination to be undertaken of the contribution by Robertson to the development of Keynes's thought, but also an assessment of the strength of Keynes's influence upon 'Robertsonian economics' to be made.

Much of the book chooses as its focus the theory of industrial fluctuation, since this is where the majority of Robertson's writings were concentrated, where he made the greatest impact upon the study of economics and where much of the debate between Robertson and Keynes took place. The discussion, however, is not restricted to the case of a *closed* economy and there is an important contribution by Thomas Humphrey (Chapter Four) which relates to the monetary approach to exchange rates to be found in Robertson's work.

NOTES

1.   A task already undertaken to some extent by Sir John R. Hicks in *Essays in Money & Interest* by D. H. Robertson, selected by J. R. Hicks (London: Fontana Library, 1966) and more recently by S. R. Dennison and J. R. Presley in *Robertson on Economic Policy* (London: Macmillan, forthcoming).

2.   There are very few other attempts to assess Sir D. H. Robertson's work other than these here. An excellent study has been published by Gordon A. Fletcher, *The Keynesian Revolution and its Critics* (London: Macmillan, 1987) and this deals extensively with Robertson's work on pages 29–180. The obituary article by P. A. Samuelson 'Sir D. H. Robertson', *Quarterly Journal of Economics*, 4, November 1963, pp. 528–36 is also worth reading, although it is unduly critical of Robertson's work.

3.   S. R. Dennison and J. R. Presley, *op. cit.*

4.   D. H. Robertson, *A Study of Industrial Fluctuation* (London: P. S. King & Son Ltd, 1915).

5.   The honour of a Fellowship of Eton College was given to him in 1948.

6.   Being a member of the ADC and the Marlowe Society.

7.   J. R. Presley, *Robertsonian Economics* (London, Macmillan, 1979).

8.   He was in fact awarded the Military Cross.

9.   Letter to the author, November 1972.

10. J. M. Keynes, *Tract on Monetary Reform* (London: Macmillan, 1923).

11. J. M. Keynes, *Treatise on Money* (London, Macmillan, 1930).

12. See also J. R. Presley (1979), *op. cit.*, Part II, Ch. 2.

13. See D. H. Robertson, *Utility and All That* (London: Allen & Unwin, 1952) p. 44.

14. D. H. Robertson, *Economic Fragments* (London: P. S. King & Son Ltd, 1931) p. 175.

15. Ibid., p. 212.

16. D. H. Robertson continued to live in Cambridge until his death in 1963.
17. D. H. Robertson, *Lectures on Economic Principles*, 3 vol. 1957–9 (London: Staples Press Ltd; paperback edition, London: Fontana Library, 1963).
18. Memorandum of Evidence submitted to the (Macmillan) Committee on Finance and Industry, April 1930.
19. Memorandum submitted to the Canadian Royal Commission on Banking and Finance, 1962; reprinted in *Essays in International Finance*, 42, May 1963, Princeton University.
20. See J. R. Dennison and J. R. Presley, *op. cit.*, Appendix II for full details.
21. J. R. Hicks, *op. cit.*
22. Unpublished introduction in a lecture in Cambridge, April 1946.
23. See pp. 127–8.
24. L. Robbins, *The Evolution of Modern Economic Theory* (London: Macmillan, pp. 248–53.
25. J. M. Keynes, *The Collected Writings of J. M. Keynes*, vols XIII and XIV, edited by D. Moggridge (London: Macmillan, published for the Royal Economic Society, 1973).

2 Dennis Robertson and the Real Business Cycle

Charles Goodhart

INTRODUCTION*

In the course of re-reading DHR's writings for this chapter, I came to believe that in his first major academic publication, the *Study of Industrial Fluctuation* (1915), Robertson had developed entirely on his own a clearly recognisable version of a Real Business Cycle theory. In Robertson's basic model, incorporating single-person entrepreneurial firms, e. g. farmers, technological shocks, notably inventions, shift intertemporal production/consumption opportunity sets, and cause producers (rationally) to vary their intertemporal supply of effort/labour. There are no market failures, no money, no fluctuations in aggregate demand in DHR's basic, stripped-down model. Of course, he subsequently extends his model to take account of the distinction between employers and employees, with the nominal wage rate of the latter being, in practice, slow to adjust; and he also then introduces, and discusses, monetary disturbances.

Nevertheless a Real Business Cycle theory lay at the core of Robertson's analysis of the Trade Cycle. Now that interest in such theories has reawakened so strongly (at least in the USA), it is worth recording, for the history of economic thought, that one of the earliest versions of such a model, if not the earliest, was developed in Cambridge

---

* I was honoured to be asked by the Master and Fellows of Trinity College, Cambridge, to give a Lecture to commemorate the Centenary of the birth of Sir Dennis Robertson (1890–1963) at Cambridge in May 1990. The remainder of this chapter is a revised version of that Lecture. My thanks are due to the Master and Fellows of Trinity College, Cambridge and especially to Robert Neild, for inviting me to give this Centenary lecture. In the preparation of this paper, I have had a great deal of help and support from Stanley Dennison, Dennis Robertson's friend, coauthor (of the new (1960) edition of *The Control of Industry*), and literary executor; and valuable advice and suggestions from Victoria Chick, Gordon Fletcher, Penelope Hatfield, Robert Neild, John Presley and Tom Wilson, none of whom are responsible for my personal interpretation of Dennis Robertson's works.

just before the First World War by a very young English academic, Dennis Holme Robertson.

Arguments to support this claim are set out on pp. 21–9. The first two Sections incorporate a more general survey of certain facets of DHR's works, as appropriate for the occasion of a Centenary contribution.

ROBERTSONIAN STYLE

> 'When I use a word', Humpty Dumpty said in rather a scornful tone, 'it means just what I choose it to mean – neither more or less.'
>
> 'The question is', said Alice, 'Whether you *can* make words mean different things.'
>
> 'The question is,' said Humpty Dumpty, 'which is to be master – that's all.'

That quotation from *Alice Through the Looking Glass* appears at the front of Chapter 2 of Robertson's Cambridge Economic Handbook on *Money*. I chose it not only because it illustrated one of Dennis's trademarks, his use of quotations from the Alice books,[1] but also because Dennis was, indeed, a master craftsman in the use of English at a time when the meaning of words such as money, savings and investment were often subject to different interpretations. He read Classics, Part 1, and remained an expert classicist. At one stage in his contribution to the symposium on 'Alternative Theories of the Rate of Interest' (*Economic Journal*, September 1937) he argued that 'It might be an advantage if all contributors to this discussion were compelled to turn their contributions into Latin prose', in order to clarify the use of words.

I would like to spend a few minutes recalling his personality and style, before turning to the *content* of selected parts of his work, particularly relating to the trade cycle. Incidentally, Holme was a family name. Two unmarried Holme sisters, Dennis's great aunts, lived next to James Meade's parents in Bath, and encouraged James to meet Dennis. Dennis played a role in encouraging him to become an economist, and was his tutor at Trinity, Cambridge, when he came over from Oxford for a year to learn the subject.

As Fritz Machlup noted in a short obituary in the Introduction to DHR's posthumously published 'A Memorandum submitted to the Canadian Royal Commission on Banking and Finance' (reprinted in *Essays in International Finance*, No 42), DHR was not only a leader of the economics profession, but 'an ornament by his style of writing, his humour and his humanism'. The carefully-wrought elegance and lucidity of his work makes it a great pleasure to re-read.

One major component of the pleasure in reading DHR's work lies in the gentle humour to be found therein, a gentleness that, however, overlaid a steadfast persistence, and indeed some bravery, (as might, perhaps, have been expected from a man who won the MC in World War One), in maintaining his own analytical position. There is very little in the analysis of his earliest works, the *Study of Industrial Fluctuation* and *Money*, that DHR ever subsequently sought to change significantly.

Dennis, the classicist and humanist, enjoyed poking fun at some of the pretensions and jargon of the subsequent generations of more mathematical economists. Let me give you two examples. The first is from *Utility and All That* (p. 40): Robertson is concerned with assessing the trade-off between possibly greater inequality today, but more growth today, tomorrow and thereafter. He writes that

> there is no difficulty, I think, about stating the problem in terms of the utilitarian calculus – let us have a little less general welfare [economic welfare in DHR's own terminology] than *might* be reaped today in order that there might not be a great deal less, but may be rather more, to-morrow and the day after and the day after that. If Samuelson likes to express the same point . . . by saying that the hypersurface of a utility-feasibility function will lie inside that of the corresponding utility-possibility function, well, that is just fine; we all have our funny little ways of putting things.

My second example is taken from the paper 'On Sticking to One's Last' (Chapter 3 in *Utility and All That*); DHR comments that

> whereas in the old days economists were generally content to indicate the *directions* in which action might be taken to promote the public good, they have latterly become much more confident about reducing

their counsel to precise and quantitative terms. It is true that some nasty tosses have been taken . . . but on the whole the practitioners of the art of predictional arithmetic appear to be pretty good . . . at coming up smiling, explaining that the connection between their variants must sometimes be taken to be stochastic rather than functional (this, as you know, is now the dignified way of saying that it is all largely a matter of guess-work after all), and returning to the charge.

This brings me briefly to the topic of DHR's views on methodology and, in particular, the use of maths. As was the common experience of economists of his generation, Dennis came to economics after having studied another subject at school and university, but unlike Keynes and several other contemporaries, DHR's speciality had been classics rather than maths. It is an indication of changing times that DHR's first book, the *Study of Industrial Fluctuation*, contained many quotations in both Latin and Greek (without translation), but not a single equation. Although it is obvious that Dennis was more proficient at maths, and certainly at understanding the mathematical analysis of others, than he liked to let on, he viewed its increasing use with considerable reservation. He felt that the need to reduce complex affairs to a simplified and tractable mathematical system tended to lead economists to concentrate unduly on a limited set of explanatory factors. Thus in his new (1948) Introduction to the 1915 *Study* DHR comments that 'my explorations . . . have left me with an abiding sense of the difficulty of providing, in a world in which so many and such various changes may be wrought by the wand of Science, neat little models of the trade cycle and (*a fortiori*) neat little packets of therapeutic pills'. Against this passage in my LSE copy, some later hand then scribbled the words, 'Kaldor, Beware!'

Although I share with DHR a congenital weakness in maths (alongside some more worthwhile experiences, such as having been editor of the Eton College Chronicle, a Fellow at Trinity College and a Professor of Banking at LSE), I have to comment that his inability, or unwillingness, to use maths at certain points in his exposition was a significant weakness. It was, however, a Cambridge tradition, at least in the first half of the twentieth century, for economists there to minimise their use of maths, and relegate it to appendices, even in those cases when they had been trained as mathematicians, viz Marshall and Keynes.

Another of Dennis' trademarks was his insistence upon teasing out the dynamic processes whereby the economy evolved, rather than relying on the comparative statics that Keynes adopted in the *General Theory*, along with many of Keynes's followers. Now I believe that Dennis' approach in this respect is likely both to be more fruitful and less likely to lead to the kind of analytical errors, for example in the analysis of the working of the multiplier and the determination of the rate of interest, of which Robertson accused Keynes. Yet if only Dennis had been able to use maths to formalize his own model, and to make it more widely accessible, he might have been able to take a more positive approach to setting out his own vision of the economic system instead of appearing, from the 1930s onwards, primarily as a critic reacting to the agenda of others, notably of course Keynes. Be that as it may, I want to revert for a moment to my final example of DHR's humour, which is to be found in his footnoted comment in his paper on 'An American "Radcliffe" Report' (*Lloyds Bank Review*, January 1962) that 'the proposition that a desirable degree of freedom is a national objective resembles somewhat, in reverse, the famous motion discussed (and decisively defeated) at a certain school debating society – "That too much athletics is a bad thing"'. I presume that the school in question was Eton. Although, or perhaps because, DHR's father had been a master at Rugby and Harrow, and Headmaster at Haileybury, he put Dennis down for an Eton scholarship. This was, indeed, fortunate. Whereas Keynes in his Introduction to DHR's *The Control of Industry* noted that there is no 'other branch of knowledge in the formation of which Englishmen can claim a more predominant part', in the course of the period from 1910 to 1939 that is still too wide a net. With Keynes, Hawtrey and Robertson all coming from the same stable, King's Scholars at Eton followed by Cambridge, it might be said that the great battles of monetary theory had their cradle in the school rooms of Eton, (with perhaps as much influence on mankind as Waterloo?).

DHR early on showed his intellectual prowess, becoming captain of the School (1907–08) and taking the Newcastle Prize (the highest classical prize) as well as many other prizes for verse and holiday exercises, on his way to a major scholarship at Trinity. He turned to economics half way through his undergraduate years here, having obtained a First in Part I of the Classics Tripos. With Keynes as his supervisor, he took Part II of the Economic Tripos in 1912, again getting a First. Keynes had been appointed Director of Studies in Economics at Trinity in 1910 (Harrod, *Life*, p. 150), but not all Trinity men were entirely happy with that. When my own father, A. L. Goodhart, arrived at Trinity in 1912 as a graduate student from Yale, intending to read economics, he was, he later told me, informed that there were doubts about how 'sound' Keynes was, and my father was encouraged to read law instead under Harry Hollond's supervision, which he did.

Despite the academic pressures of working for a First in Economics in two years, DHR nevertheless found the time to become President of the Union, President of the Cambridge University Liberal Club, and President of the Amateur Dramatic Club (ADC), as well as winning the Chancellor's Medal for English Verse, for the third time running, *all in 1911*. He continued with his dramatic activities until 1930, mainly with the Marlowe Society, but he continued to write verse throughout his life. While I should have wished to have had the time to talk more about his love of life at Trinity, (the Trinity cats as well as the Fellows), I shall conclude this Section with a rendition of Dennis's 'A Non-econometricians's Lament' from the Appendix of Economic Commentaries.

> As soon as I could safely toddle
> My parents handed me a model.
> My brisk and energetic pater
> Provided the accelerator,
> My mother, with her kindly gumption,
> The function guiding my consumption.
> And every week I had from her
> A lovely new parameter,
> With lots of little leads and lags
> In pretty parabolic bags.
>
> With optimistic expectation
> I started on my explorations,

And swore to move without a swerve
Along my sinusoidal curve.
Alas! I knew how it would end;
I've mixed the cycle and the trend,
And fear that, growing daily skinnier,
I have at length become non-linear.
I wander glumly round the house
As though I were exogenous,
And hardly capable of feeling
The difference 'tween floor and ceiling.
I scarcely know, a pallid ghost,
Can tell ex ante from ex post;
My thoughts are sadly inelastic,
My acts incurably stochastic.

ROBERTSON'S MAJOR WORK

I shall turn now from his style to the coverage and content of Robertson's academic work. Any taxonomic classification is inherently somewhat arbitrary, but I would divide his work into five major categories, these being in rough order of the timing in which he first addressed these studies of: (1) trade cycles; (2) industrial structure; (3) monetary economics; (4) microeconomics/(utility and value); and (5) macroeconomic commentary and policy advice. I have made a tentative allocation of his books and main papers under these separate headings, though some fall into more than one category, in the attached table. While rough and ready, the table does, I think, fairly record the basic shape of the changing pattern of DHR's work. This began with the study of the determinants of the trade cycle, but his interest in this, or at least in his own original approach to this subject, and waned after the 1920s, apart from an occasional survey-type essay on current developments in trade cycle theory.

There were, next, two somewhat minor themes in Dennis' academic work, being respectively, first, his work on industrial structure, as represented mainly by his Cambridge handbook on *The Control of Industry* and his involvement in the 'Empty Boxes' debate in the 1920s, and, second, his work on microeconomics, in which his first two volumes of Lectures (1963) is the most sustained study, but his doughty defence of cardinal utility, (in a field of ferocious technical complexity), is perhaps best known.

Dennis did not begin his academic career as a monetary economist; indeed, as I shall record shortly, his view was that the trade cycle was a real, not a monetary, phenomenon. Indeed he was even pitchforked to a degree into monetary economics, since Keynes himself had initially intended to write the Cambridge Economic Handbook on money, but, being too busy had turned the job over to Dennis.[2] Be that as it may, Robertson, initially in collaboration with Keynes, but increasingly during the 1930s in disagreement with Keynes, took a major role in the debates and development of Cambridge monetary theory. Personally for DHR, the disagreements with Keynes, and, even more so, conflicts with his followers, were a source of considerable unhappiness, but analytically this period represented the high point of his theoretical work. I can still remember that, on the one occasion when I met DHR personally, for tea in his rooms at Trinity, I asked him, being a callow undergraduate, whether his disputes with Keynes had been 'exciting'. The deep sadness of his reply still evokes in me a feeling of shame for my boorish behaviour.

When DHR was writing his first books, the *Study of Industrial Fluctuation* and *Money*, the world was, or had until recently been, linked by the gold standard. With this system having worked successfully until 1914, Dennis was able to treat the real world economy as a unity, though the emphasis that he placed on the terms of trade between industry and agriculture, and on the industrial importance of shipping and shipbuilding, showed his awareness and concern with international economic issues. Thereafter he wrote several papers on international monetary issues in the inter-war period, (1924, 1930, 1938). Then at the start of the war he took up a position as economic adviser to Sir Frederick Phillips, Third Secretary of the Treasury, covering the field of overseas finance and the balance of payments; and in this role he participated in the Bretton Woods negotiations, during which there was some reconciliation with Keynes; though he had remained *personally* on quite good terms with him throughout.

TABLE 1   *The allocation by subject of Robertson's work*

(1) Trade cycle	(2) Industrial structure	(3) Monetary economics	(4) Microeconomics	(5) Macroeconomics commentary and policy
A Study of Industrial Fluctuation (1915)	*The Control of Industry* (1923)	*Money* (1922)	*Economic Fragments* (1937) Section 1, 1 and 3	*Economic Fragments* (1931) Section I, 2, and Section III, 2 and 3.
Banking Policy and the Price Level Chpts I–IV	*Economic Fragments* (1931) Section II.	*Banking Policy and the Price Level* (1926), Chpts V–VIII	*Essays in Monetary Theory* (1940) Chpts 14–16	*Economic Essays and Addresses*, (1931), Pt. I Chpts, 2, 4, 5
Economic Fragments (1931) Section III, 1.	'Those Empty Boxes', *Economic Journal*, (1924)	*Economic Essays and Addresses* (1931) Pt. II, Chpts 1–3.	*Utility and All That* (1952) Chpts 1, 3, 4.	*Utility and All That* (1952), Chpts 2, 8–13.
Economic Essays and Addresses (1931) Pt. II, Chpts 2, 3.	'Increasing Returns and the Representative Firm', *Economic Journal*, (1930)	*Essays in Monetary Theory* (1940) Chpts 1–4, 6, 9, 11, 12	*Economic Commentaries* (1956), Chpts 1, 2.	*Britain in the World Economy* (1953).
Essays in Monetary Theory (1940) Chpts 5, 7, 10, 13.		*Utility and All That* (1952) Chpts 5–7, 14–16.	*Lectures on Economic Principles*, Vols 1 and 2 (1963)	*Economic Commentaries* (1956) Chpts 6–10.
'A Spanish Contribution to the Theory of Fluctuations', *Economica* (1940)		*Economic Commentaries* (1956) Chpts 3, 4.	'Welfare Criteria: An Exchange of Notes' *Economic Journal* (1962)	*Growth, Wages, Money* (1960)

TABLE 1 (cont'd)

(1) Trade cycle	(2) Industrial structure	(3) Monetary economics	(4) Microeconomics	(5) Macroeconomics commentary and policy
Utility and All That (1952) Chpt 15.		*Lectures on Economic Principles* (1963), Vol. 3		*Essays in Money and Interest* (1966) Chpts 1
Economic Commentaries (1956) Chpt 5.				*Cohen Council on Prices Productivity and Incomes* First Report (1957)*
Essays in Money and Interest (1966) Chpts 4, 6–8.		*Memorandum to Canadian Royal Commission on Banking and Finance,* (1963).		Many of DHR's post-war writings, unallocated above, including his final six unpublished ones, fall into this category.
		Essays in Money and Interest (1963) Chpts 1–3, 5, 9–17.		
		Most of DHR's other published works, not otherwise recorded here, between 1931 and 1938 were on monetary economics, mostly involving DHR's disagreement with Keynes.		

* Professor S. R. Dennison has informed me that evidence exists, in the shape of letters from the other members of the Council to DHR, indicating that this Report was primarily drafted by Robertson.

The combination of his early work on the trade cycle, and his subsequent knowledge of domestic and international monetary matters, gave DHR a wide and thorough appreciation of economic issues. This, together with his sage and balanced judgement, led DHR to be increasingly called upon to comment upon the current macro-economic policy issues of the day. Thus many of his later post-war papers take the form of wise comment on policy issues.

In his book on *Robertsonian Economics*, John Presley passes over DHR's industrial and micro-economic contributions to economics, and I shall follow his example here. At the heading of Chapter 1 to *The Control of Industry* DHR has the following Alice quotation, "'Ahem!" said the Mouse, with an important air. "Are you all ready? This is the driest thing I know. Silence all round".' I think that that is unfair as regards *The Control of Industry*, but apt indeed as a comment on the welfare/utility measurement debate. Anyhow I am incapable, incompetent and short of time to get involved in any discussion of DHR's microeconomics.

There is no question but that it is Robertson's contributions to the development of Cambridge monetary economics for which he will be best remembered. But again I shall not discuss that much further here, for two main reasons. First, he will be remembered for this work. Just as economists are continually being drawn back to reconsider and reassess the debate between the banking and currency schools, so they will continue to be drawn back to the Cambridge monetary controversies of the 1920s and 1930s, and, as the Dodo said, 'All must have prizes'.

Indeed, such reassessment has been a continuing process. In that context I think, perhaps, first of Tsiang,[3] who through the years has advanced Robertsonian lines of argument, but also of the papers by Tom Wilson,[4] Hicks,[5] Harry Johnson,[6] Fellner,[7] and more recently by Bridel,[8] Kohn,[9] Fletcher,[10] and of course, John Presley's major study on *Robertsonian Economics*.[11] This listing, moreover, is far from comprehensive, only covering those works coming recently to my own attention. Some, Tom Wilson for example, fear that Dennis' contributions to monetary economics may become overlooked. I see no likelihood at all of that. My second reason for passing *this* opportunity to discuss Robertson's monetary theory is that I have already had the chance to compare his and Keynes's theories in my contribution to the Eighth Keynes Seminar in 1987 on *Keynes, Money and Monetarism*,[12] and I would not want to repeat myself.

There are, however, just a couple of brief points that I should like to make now. First, Fletcher, in his book on *The Keynesian Revolution and its Critics*, in which Dennis is cast as chief critic, seizes[13] upon a single invalid footnote in Presley's major study on *Robertsonian Economics*,[14] to claim that Robertson 'failed to understand the nature of saving and the "paradox of thrift"'. Robertson however, emphasized[15] that he was the first economist to attack the 'Treasury view' in his earliest 1915 book, commenting that 'That whole point is that in times of depression savings are not otherwise so applied', [to the creation of capital],[16] and he went on to develop the theory 'that under certain conditions the process of individual saving, so far from finding vent in the accumulation of useful stocks, may become completely abortive'. Moreover, DHR understood the mechanics of the multiplier perfectly well,[17] and indeed felt it necessary to expand on the dynamic *process* involved, rather than just reply, as Keynes sometimes did, on the comparative static outcome.

My own reading of this facet of the debate is not that Robertson did not understand 'the paradox of thrift', but that he assumed a different ordering of events. Dennis regarded output as being inelastic in supply in the very short run, the Robertsonian day, so when demand shifted, as the propensity to spend out of *yesterday's* income (the Robertsonian lag) varied, the first effect had to be on the price level. Such price changes led automatically to forced and automatic saving, and also to associated movements in the somewhat idiosyncratic Robertsonian concepts of lacking and stinting, when prices went up, and their reserve when prices went down, and also to (a Pigouvian real-balance type) induced saving, lacking and stinting, all of which tended to offset the effect on quantities of the shift in demand. It was only at the second stage that the shift in demand, and of the change in prices to which it gave rise, led on to a change in real output.[18]

Within his own framework of assumptions, DHR's logic strikes me as impeccable. But, while I would agree that output is in inelastic supply in the very short run, the weakness of DHR's position is that he fails to appreciate sufficiently that initially shifts in demand will be met by fluctuations in inventories at given prices, rather then by price changes.[19] Whereas Dennis' criticisms of Keynes's work are, in my view, mostly well-taken he himself can, I believe, be criticized for not giving enough weight to the critical role of inventory adjustment, for example as argued by Hawtrey and Harrod, in causing fluctuations in nominal expenditures to impinge initially on real output rather than on prices. Even when directly attacked on this point, Dennis tended to duck the issue.

Now I think there is room for argument about Mr Hawtrey's views on the relative practical importance and the time-sequence of the various possible methods of response to an alteration in consumer's demand – alteration of prices, alteration of output and alteration of stocks. But I would plead rather that analysis on my plane of abstraction has the advantage of setting in high relief the two things which analytically are of fundamental interest – first, the way in which an act of economy on the part of individuals can go to waste without eventuating in the formation of material capital; and secondly, the nature of the forces diffusing the operation of this process through time. (DHR, "Mr Robertson on 'Saving and Hoarding'", *Economic Journal*, December 1933, p. 712).

My second point concerns liquidity preference. Of the three margins on which the rate of interest operates, the productivity of capital, the propensity to save and the demand for liquidity, Keynes gave extreme emphasis to the last. But this margin depends on an institutional quirk, that liquid money balances bear a below-market, in fact generally zero, interest rate. We now, of course, realize that chequeable sight deposits can, and now often do, offer a market-based yield; and, it is also technically quite possible to offer such a yield on currency.[20] When *all* money bears market-related interest, the amount of money held would rise until the demand for liquidity was satiated. The third margin would just disappear; but the rate of interest would not fall to zero; nor would it in a non-monetary Crusoe economy. As DHR always emphasized, liquidity preference can be, often is, of primary importance in the short run, but its influence fades away in the medium and longer term.

ROBERTSON'S TRADE CYCLE THEORY

Although Dennis will continue to be best known as a monetary economist, I would contend that his early work on the trade cycle deserves
almost as significant a niche in the history of economic thought. As
Ashton wrote in his delightful review[21] of the reprinted 1948 issue of
DHR's *Study of Industrial Fluctuation*, that, before then, economists
made their 'own choice between competing explanations of the trade
cycle, labelled variously "climatic" "psychological", and "monetary"'.
Dennis, instead, emphasized fluctuations in the marginal efficiency of
investment, largely driven by technological inventions and innovations.
Indeed he, along with Schumpeter, who were working independently
of each other, may be described as the original forerunners of *real*
business cycle theory.

Ashton again notes that 'We knew [in 1914] that investment (which
was identified with saving) had something to do with these [oscillat-
ions], but we were not at all clear that it lays at the heart of the matter
. . . it was this work written by a Cambridge don in his early twenties,
that provided us with our *Novum Organum*'. It was, indeed, a remarkable effort of youthful prodigy. Within two years of gaining his First
in economics, at the age of twenty-four, Robertson had collected
an enormous mass of empirical and historical data (if somewhat un-
digested by modern standards), from which he shaped a new and original theory. There were even occasions when DHR might have had
his leg pulled in his pursuit of facts, c.f. the following passage from
Study, p. 197, n. 1:

I have been told that the diminished consumption of beer since 1900
is partly due to the attractions and increased cheapness of bananas as
a good and occupation [sic!] on public holidays: and the diminution
in the rate of increase of the imports of this fruit in 1906, accompanied by higher prices, the actual decrease in 1907 and again in 1910
is certainly curious when compared with the beer consumption curve.

This *Study of Industrial Fluctuation* was the thesis on which he
obtained his Fellowship at Trinity in 1914, and it was published in the
following year, 1915. Dennis was rightly proud of this effort, which
he later described as 'a crude and primitive attempt to set theory and

history walking hand in hand'.[22] It was, however, to be DHR's sole serious excursion into empirical applied work. Given the skill in interweaving facts and theory demonstrated in the *Study*, this must be viewed as a disappointment.

After a preliminary chapter setting out 'Definitions' and justifying the existence and importance of cycles as a subject worthy of study, Robertson discusses in Part 1 the factors affecting first the supply of individual trades, Chapters 1 to 3, and then the demand for these same individual trades. As condensed subsequently in his 1926 *Banking Policy and the Price Level*, the early chapters of which essentially involve a prècis of the theoretical parts of the earlier *Study*, the factors that

> offer a rational incentive to an industrial group to alter the scale of its output [are]: (1) an alteration in its real operating cost; (2) an alteration in the intensity of its desire for the goods which it receives in exchange for its products; (3) an alteration in the 'real demand price' for its products, that is, in the rate at which other industries are prepared to part with their products in exchange for its own.[23]

DHR reckoned that cost efficiency was more likely to occur during periods of industrial depression.

> During the later stages of a 'depression' there is, generally speaking, a progressive advance in the effectiveness of labour, a progressive writing off of inflated capital charges. During the later stages of a 'boom' there is a progressive recourse to inferior instruments of production, a progressive utilization of over-tired labour, wasteful methods of management, and inferior business leadership. (*Banking Policy*, p. 9; also see *Study*, especially pp. 125–9).

Again costs could go down because of a cheapening of an important input, notably agricultural raw materials. Much of the fluctuation in the intensity of desire of producers in one industry for the products of another, and hence in variations in relative real demand prices, would depend on the vagaries of fashion, but some would have a more general effect, e.g. war, shifts in food prices, and above all inventions and innovations, which would both add to the demand for the new products, and where such products were also capital inputs into other industries, prospectively lower the costs in these other industries.

Most of the specific inventions mentioned by DHR in the *Study*, to wit railways, basic steel, electricity and oil[24] were largely, or primarily, capital goods (or instrumental goods to use DHR's terminology) but a sufficiently important invention in a purely consumer goods industry (e.g. motor cars) could have produced a general upsurge in output, through three routes: first, an increase in demand for cars (and their components); second, by the accelerator effect from an expanding car industry on the demand for factories and plant to build cars;[25] and third, by an increased effort/output in other industries in order to obtain command over the new product.

Robertson sets his analysis initially in a non-monetary world of individual producers (without employed labour).[26] In such a setting he asks himself how can there be an aggregate fluctuation in output and prices; will not Say's Law hold? His answer to that is that a significant technological, or exogenous, improvement, e.g. in agricultural production, or an invention will give these individual producers more command, for the time being, over a desired instrumental or consumption good. Provided that the demand for this new cheaper (in real terms) product is elastic in terms of own-effort,[27] each individual producer will increase his own input, so aggregate output will rise.

DHR was as sparing with his graphical illustrations as he was with his algebra, but there is one diagram, to illustrate the above analysis, that appears first on p. 132 of *Study*, but then is repeated several times both in *Study* and *Banking Policy*. It clearly played such a central position in his thought that it is worth reproducing (Figure 1). Units of effort are measured along OX, units of utility along OY. In state 1, the equilibrium demand, in terms of own effort, for the product subject to exogenous (technological) change is OA. The marginal utility of all other goods is measured by UU^1, and the marginal disability of effort by EE^1. In State 2, after the technological invention, the product concerned has cheapened; *assuming* that the own-effort demand is elastic for that product, the new equilibrium demand for it will shift out to OA^1, thereby shifting out the UU^1 curve to U^1U^1, and raising total output and production depending on the slopes of the UU^1 and EE^1 curves.

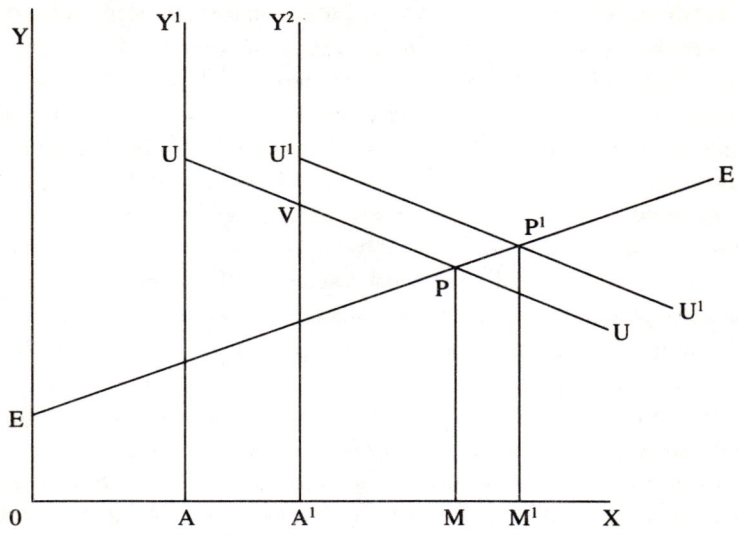

Figure 1

We are now in a position to examine his theory of 'Fluctuations of General Trade', which forms Part 2 of the *Study*. Robertson breaks into the cycle, admittedly somewhat arbitrarily, at the point of revival from depression.[28] His analysis of the forces leading to this revival are succinctly summarised in his concluding chapter, p. 239, as subject to 'the following influences':

(1) A general increase in the physical productivity of effort due to the adoption of improved methods, etc, under the stimulus of depression; (2) an increase, due to an increased bounty of nature, in the exchange value of industrial products against the products of agriculture; and (3) an increase in the expected future productivity of constructional goods, due either (i) to the wearing out of an exceptionally large number of existing instruments, (ii) to the discovery of the industrial possibility of a new country, or (iii) to some physical or legal invention.

From among this varied set of possible causes, Robertson always gave pride of place to technological inventions. (The role of agricultural fluctuations was still important in 1914, but steadily diminished as the century progressed.) By definition such inventions are (normally) not predictable in advance. Thus there is a tendency for most economists and commentators to be excessively pessimistic about the possibility of recovery from depression, a point that Robertson made on several occasions in later life. 'It is possible, I think, to be too gloomy. At no point has it been possible to divine just where the spring of "demand for waiting" would gush forth in the coming years.' (from 'Mr Keynes and the Rate of Interest', Chapter XIII, *Essays in Money and Interest*, p. 184).

Once recovery had started, especially when in response to inventions and innovations of the kind mentioned, there would then be an upsurge in the demand for constructional, investment goods, for DHR was well aware that the oscillations of the trade cycle were concentrated in the capital goods industries. The length and extent of this upsurge depended on the gestation period and size, or indivisibility, and specificity, (or intractability, to use Dennis' terminology) of the main new investment projects, e.g. railways, electrical generation and distribution systems, oil refineries, etc. In general Robertson believed that there would be a tendency for over-investment at this stage, in the sense that more of the new equipment would be ordered than could subsequently be profitably employed. This was partly because of the ignorance of individual entrepreneurs of the plans of others, partly because each entrepreneur, even if aware of the likelihood of aggregate over-investment, could still profit if he could get the new equipment into production early,[29] and partly because of the dynamic, optimistic nature of capitalist entrepreneurs, with the quote from Walt Whitman with which Dennis opens and concludes his *Study*.

Urge and urge and urge
Always the procreant urge of the world.

As the boom progresses inefficiencies and rising costs return, and a bad harvest may halt the upturn, but DHR focuses rather on two other possible causes for its termination. The first is an under-saving hypothesis.[30] With too little saving, too few stocks of consumption goods to make available to investment goods' producers, it becomes physically impossible to maintain the output of investment goods: and the price of non-constructional goods may rise relative to that of constructional goods.[31] Robertson, at times, added yet another possible cause for a downturn, arising from a distributional shift in income receipts to the profits of the rich during booms; 'For rich people have less need to spend up to the hilt than poor people; hence sooner or later the rate of increase in the demand for consumption goods will decline, and with it will decline the incentive to purchase capital goods even on the existing scale'. ('A Survey of Modern Monetary Controversy', Chapter IX in *Essays in Money and Interest*, p. 117; also see *Study*, pp. 237–8.)

Robertson felt that such under-saving had indeed been responsible for some of the upper turning-points of historical cycles, notably the crisis of 1907,[32] but it was not invariably the cause of down-turn. But if under-saving did not stop the cycle, then Robertson was confident that over-investment would; this was the essential cause of downturn in investment demand. Thus 'the relapse in constructional industry is seen to be due to the existence or imminence of over-production of instrumental as compared with consumable goods'.[33] Apart from the tendency to over-invest in the boom, all this is perfectly rational.

> Consumable goods may be abundant, but if it is known that with the close of the period of gestation they are about to become far more abundant still, a wise community will devote them to eliciting the immediate production of other consumable rather than of constructional goods. The fundamental meaning of over investment is failure to attain the ideal distribution of the community's income of consumable goods through time. (*Study*, p. 180)

With the investment boom having been punctured, the Robertsonian individual producers then tend to draw in their horns, and reduce output even of consumption goods. But this is not due to some form of market failure and price stickiness; indeed DHR spends some time attacking the under-consumption theory of J. A. Hobson on the grounds that price declines would restore real demand.[34] This latter argument is asserted, rather than fully worked out, in the *Study*, but extended to incorporate Pigouvian real balance effects in *Banking Policy*. Thus 'Suppose that some or all of the public, their incomes not having suffered any change, experience an increased desire to hoard . . . the result would be a fall in the price-level, and an unexpectedly increased consumption on the part of some members of the public'.[35] No, the general decline in output, even in the consumer goods industry, is due to elasticity of effort of the Robertsonian producers in the face of shifting technological possibilities.

> Supposing it were physically possible for the human race to maintain its productive efforts throughout the whole twenty-four hours of everyday, would it be to its economic advantage to do so? . . . the aim of economic endeavour is [not] to maximise the gross satisfaction derived from the consumption of goods, instead of the excess of this satisfaction over the aggregate dissatisfaction involved by all kinds of effort and sacrifice . . . the operation of industry in general on the full scale rendered physically possible by the previous orgy of investment may involve a 'general over-production' in a very real and genuine sense. (*Study*, p. 200)

Robertson's approach in this respect is very closely akin to those of modern purveyors of 'real business cycle' theory, such as Kydland, Long, Plosser, Prescott *et al.*[36] Since some may not be familiar with this line of analysis, let me explain further. The opportunity set facing the independent Robertsonian producers has now contracted, because the overproduction of capital goods has reduced producers' command over *future* consumer goods from an investment of income from work. Since the alternative of using their time in leisure pursuits, in golf or politics for example, remains as attractive as ever, the producers will choose to shift part of their available time from work to play. 'When trade is bad he is, owing to his comfortable circumstances and his addiction to gentlemanly pursuits such as golf and politics, readier even than the workman who is assured of full employment, and far readier than the workman who is threatened or visited with the loss of his job, to contract both his effort and his consumption' (*Banking Policy*, p. 20). The reduction in output is, therefore, a supply-side, not a demand-determined phenomenon in such models.

There is, indeed, one further twist to the real business cycle approach which Dennis expounded, which has not yet, to my knowledge, been rediscovered by our more recent theorists. This is that there may be a systematic difference in the elasticities of supply and effort between entrepreneurs, whose supply is more elastic owing to a wider range of non-work opportunities, and workers. 'In times of boom in any trade the high value attached to leisure by the manual workers is a factor which operates to restrict production below the level at which the business man desires to maintain it' (*Study*, p. 207, also see *Economic Fragments*, the paper on 'Economic Incentive', on 'The Slump in Shipping and Shipbuilding', especially p. 122, and on 'The Stabilization of Employment', especially pp. 133–4).

This difference leads to 'disharmony' between the objectives of capital and labour. Such disharmony might, one might have thought, have been mitigated by the working of the price mechanism, in that the combination of a fluctuating demand and inelastic supply of wage-labour would have led to extreme fluctuations in wages. But Robertson could see that institutional arrangements, e. g. contracts fixed in money (not real) terms,[37] brought about 'the lagging of money wages behind rising prices . . . now so generally admitted as scarcely to require detailed illustration'.[38] This led to an insufficiency of labour, and a shift of incomes from wages to profits, in the boom, and to involuntary unemployment, and a shift of incomes to labour in the slump.

> Moreover, when the situation is thus reversed [in the slump], the business classes will be in a better position to enforce their control of industrial policy. For while an employer cannot easily compel a workman to work more than he wishes to, he can, through his control of the access to the instruments of production, effectively prevent him from working as much as he wishes to. It follows that the complaints of involuntary unemployment among the wage-earners need not make us doubt the correctness, as far as concerns the business classes, and therefore the course of industrial policy, of our diagnosis of the industrial malady. It follows also that no solution of the problem can be completely satisfactory which aims merely at the fulfilment of the policy which the enlightened self-interest of the business classes would dictate, and neglects the genuine want of

harmony between that interest and the interest of the working classes. (*Study*, pp. 210–11)

In terms of its significance for the framework of his *basic* theory, Dennis saw much wage stickiness as involving only a minor qualification,[39] but its *practical* importance was, and remains, vital. Dennis would, however, never have got himself tied up over the question of whether real wages fluctuated pro or contra-cyclically, since there were two forces operating against each other, first technological fluctuations in productivity, and second institutional shifts between wages and profits, so that *any* pattern of real wage fluctuation over the cycle would be admissible.

Note that the analysis so far has been conducted entirely in a non-monetary framework. Dennis had been encouraged (by Pigou) to dig down below the monetary surface to get at the real forces involved in trade cycles,[40] and DHR became a fervent believer that cycles were primarily caused by real forces. In the *Study* money makes no appearance until page 211 out of a book of 254 pages. He was later to write that 'if I have a personal heresy in these matters, it is that in recent years, alike in academic, financial and political circles, we have heard rather too much about that entity [the rate of interest] in connection with the processes of trade recovery and recession'.[41]

DHR was perfectly well aware of the possibility of fluctuations in credit expansion, which could aggravate the business cycle, caused by inappropriate shifts in either the gold monetary base[42] or in the confidence of bankers, but he tended to see these as playing normally a secondary role to the real forces involved. Moreover, with such real forces exerting their influence initially on prices rather than on output, the existence of a large stock of nominally fixed money balances provided, as DHR described in detail in *Banking Policy*, an offsetting source of stability via both automatic and induced real balance effects.

CONCLUSION

I hope that I have done enough to persuade you that Robertson should be regarded as one of the progenitors of real business cycle theory, and indeed of a theoretical position that was both clear and subtle. You should, however, note the *practical* importance of his qualification to the effect that wages were *not* perfectly flexible, and hence involuntary unemployment would occur during depressions.

At the time, his proposed remedies for curing the depression were quite radical and advanced, including public works and the (quiet) accumulation of buffer stocks by the government, in addition to the collection and publication of data on investment intentions.[43] Yet DHR was a conservative at heart in several respects. First, he wished to conserve and build upon the foundations of economic analysis constructed by his earlier masters, Marshall and Pigou, and he was horrified by Keynes's iconoclasm in this respect. Second, he became increasingly doubtful about entrusting the power and oversight over economic decisions into the single hands of the state. Perhaps his favourite quote from Alice was

> ''Tis love, 'tis love', said the Duchess, 'that makes the world go round.' 'Somebody said', whispered Alice, 'that it's done by everybody minding their own business.' 'Ah well', replied the Duchess, 'It means much the same thing.'[44]

Again, he felt that the primary function of monetary policy should be to achieve general price stability, which could in turn be achieved by sufficiently vigorous use of the interest rate instrument, and that the post-war commitment of full employment was pitched at an unrealistic and unattainable level. Thus he commented that 'any nation which gives its mind to it can create [balance of payments] difficulties for itself in half an hour with the aid of the printing press and a strong trade union movement'.[45] For expressing such opinions in a gentle and mild manner, the odd 'Squeak from Aunt Sally', he was excoriated by the more fashionable economists of the day.

And yet, as Dennis noted, 'highbrow opinion is like a hunted hare; if you stand in the same place, or nearly the same place, it can be relied to come round to you in a circle'.[46] For reasons that should be obvious that is one of my own favourite quotations. But Dennis was always a pragmatist rather than an idealogue, and he would, I am sure, have been just as doubtful of the excesses of the neoclassical as he was of the

Keynesian Revolution. For example, he preferred the pegged Bretton Woods system to a system of flexible exchange rates, it being a case to his mind of

> And always keep a hold of nurse
> For fear of finding something worse.[47]

Again he clearly had doubts whether the assumption of rational expectations was generally tenable:

> The economist . . . has often been accused of using a crude and obsolete psychology, assuming without good cause that in the ordinary business of life men seek their own interests, and seek them intelligently, whereas it is clear in fact that, in the first place, they often act unreflectingly, under the influence of sudden impulse or of ingrained custom, and secondly, that they are often influenced by altruism or public spirit. (*Lectures on Economic Principles*, vol. 1 p. 23)

He would surely have had some gentle fun in exposing the extremes to which such theory has been taken in recent decades; and in his only comment on the subject he came down firmly on the side of discretion rather than rules in the conduct of monetary policy.[48]

Dennis always liked to maintain a balance, leaning against the current fashion, sometimes a somewhat tyrannical fashion, of the day. His favourite analogy for his own position was, I believe, that of the tightrope walker Blondin, to maintain a sensible balance amongst the competing pressures and theories.[49]

NOTES

1. A usage that led the occasional student to wonder whether the Alice books were required economic textbooks. Professor S. R. Dennison records a letter from an Indian student to DHR to that effect.
2. Robertson told this to Stanley Dennison, who is my own source here.
3. See, for example, 'Liquidity Preference and Loanable Funds Theories,

Multiplier and Velocity Analyses: A Synthesis', *American Economic Review*, 46, September 1956), and 'Keynes's Finance Demand for Liquidity, Robertson's Loanable Funds Theory and Friedman's Monetarism', *Quarterly Journal of Economics*, 94, May 1980.

4.   *Economic Journal*, September 1953, and *Journal of Economic Literature*, 1990.

5.   Introduction to *Essays in Money and Interest* (1966), *Economica*, 1942, *Greek Economic Review*, 1986.

6.   *Review of Economic Studies*, 1951–2.

7.   *American Economic Review*, (1952)

8.   *Cambridge Monetary Thought* (Macmillan: London, 1987)

9.   See, for example, Meir Kohn, 'A Loanable Funds Theory of Unemployment and Monetary Disequilibrium', *American Economic* Review, 71, December 1981; 'Policy Effectiveness and the Specification of Effective Demand: Keynes Rescued by Robertson', Dartmouth College, mimeo (1985); 'Monetary Analysis, The Equilibrium Method, and Keynes's "General Theory"', *Journal of Political Economy*, 94, December 1986.

10. *The Keynesian Revolution and its Critics* (Macmillan: London, 1989).

11. (Macmillan: London, 1978).

12. Ed. R. Hill (Macmillan: London, 1989). My paper on 'Keynes and Monetarism' occurs in Session 2, pp. 106–20.

13. p. 45 and n. 55.

14. p. 182, n. 18.

15. *A Study of Industrial Fluctuation* (1948) 'Introduction'; p. XV.

16. Ibid.; also *Banking Policy and the Price Level*, pp. 45–6, 96–7; also see H. G. Johnson, Ibid. p. 98, and DHR's reply, 'Comments on Mr Johnson's Notes', *Review of Economic Studies*, 19, 1951–2, pp. 105–10, especially p. 108.

17. See the table on p. 143 in 'Effective Demand and the Multiplier', Chapter 11 in *Essays in Money and Interest*.

18. See 'Theories of Banking Policy', esp 28, Chapter 1 in *Essays in Money and Interest*; 'Saving and Hoarding', Chapter 3 in Ibid.; also 'Mr Keynes's Theory of Money', p. 410, footnote 1, *Economic Journal*, XII (163), September 1931, pp. 395–411.

19. Also see his short comment in 'Alternative Theories of the Rate of Interest' *Economic Journal*, 47 (187), September 1937, p. 429.

20. For example, by offering prizes in a lottery based on the serial numbers of outstanding notes; there have been some actual historical occasions of positive-yielding currency issues. The latest of these to come to my attention are the notes issued by the US Treasury, authorized by Acts of Congress 3 March, 1861, and 30 June 1864, with 6 per cent interest compounded semi-annually, as recorded in J. Stevenson's note on 'Coins', New York *Sunday Times*, 11 March 1990. My thanks are due to Mr S. Hauptman for sending me the column.

21. 'Industrial Fluctuation', *Economica*, August 1951, pp. 298–302, quotation from p. 298.
22. Taken from *Utility and All That*, p. 192; in the opening page of 'New Light on an Old Story', Chapter 15 in the above.
23. *Banking Policy*, pp. 8/9.
24. 'New Introduction', pp. IX/X.
25. Presley interprets DHR as being sceptical 'of the importance of the acceleration principle in causing macro-industrial revival', *Robertsonian Economics*, p. 60. My reading of this, especially *Study*, p. 125, is that the net effects depend on whether the increased demand/output for one branch of consumption goods is balanced by a reduced demand/output from other branches, and this latter depends on the third factor discussed above.
26. On this, see the entry on 'Robertson' by Danes in *New Palgrave*.
27. DHR treats this as the normal case, but accepts that there may be exceptions to the rule.
28. Chapter 1, Part II.
29. 'The interest of the owner [is] in securing rapid delivery of his ship at almost any cost before the freight market breaks, in the hope of recouping himself in a few months for a large part of its capital costs, and perhaps selling it at the psychological moment' ('The Slump in Shipping and Shipbuilding', *Economic Fragments*, p. 122).
30. *Study*, Part II, Chapter II, Section 2, pp. 170–80.
31. Ibid., p. 174.
32. New Introduction to the *Study*, p. XIII.
33. *Study*, p. 187, also see pp. 180–9.
34. Ibid., pp. 236/7.
35. *Banking Policy*, p. 53.
36. See, for example, C. I. Plosser, 'Understanding Real Business Cycles', *Journal of Economic Perspectives*, 3, Summer 1989; J. B. Long and C. I. Plosser, 'Real Business Cycles', *Journal of Political Economy*, 91, February 1983; F. Kydland and E. C. Prescott, 'Time to Build and Aggregate Fluctuations', *Econometrica*, 50, November 1982.
37. *Study*, p. 213.
38. Ibid., p. 215.
39. *Study*, p. 210.
40. New Introduction to the *Study*, pp. xii/xiii.
41. 'A Survey of Modern Monetary Controversy' (1937), reprinted as Chapter IX in *Essay in Money and Interest*; quote from p. 118.
42. See the section on 'Gold – Medicine, Poison and Intoxicant' Section 4, Chapter III, Part II in the *Study*, pp. 228–35.
43. See section 3 of Chapter 4 (Conclusion) of Part II on I 'Remedies – The Depression'. In addition, DHR was undecided whether the advantage of cartelisation in stabilizing investment and prices over the cycle outweighed their other disadvantages.

44.   From 'What does the Economist Economize', Chapter IX in *Economic Commentaries*; quote from p. 154.
45.   From *Britain in the World Economy*, p. 56, originally from 'The Economic Outlook', Chapter 2 in *Utility and All That*, p. 56.
46.   From 'Thoughts on Meeting some important Persons', Chapter IV in *Economic Commentaries*; quote from p. 81.
47.   *Memorandum submitted to the Canadian Royal Commission on Banking and Finance*, p. 30.
48.   In his review of Lloyd Mints' book on *Monetary Policy for a Competitive Society*, originally in the *American Economic Review*, June 1951, reprinted as 'Stable Money', Chapter 16, in *Utility and All That*, pp. 201–5.
49.   In 'A Survey of Modern Monetary Controversy', Chapter IX in *Essays in Money and Interest*.

3 Robertson, Money, and Monetarism[1]

Thomas Wilson

I

Of the great economists of the twentieth century, there is, perhaps, none whose work is now more neglected than Dennis Robertson. This neglect might be understandable – though not, from a scholarly standpoint, justifiable – if Robertson had been concerned only with topics that are no longer of interest to economists; but this, of course, was not the case. If the views of J. M. Keynes still deserve close attention, those of D. H. Robertson cannot properly be set aside as unimportant and irrelevant. For many years the two worked closely together at Cambridge, each much influenced in developing his ideas by what the other was doing. Austin Robinson has observed that Keynes regarded Robertson as 'the keeper of his conscience. If he could convince Dennis, he felt that he was right'.[2] This was an important role but it was not his only one, for Robertson's own creative contributions were at times ahead of Keynes's own thinking. Did not Keynes, himself, describe Hawtrey and Robertson as respectively, his 'grandparent and parent in the paths of errancy'?[3] Although in the thirties their ideas diverged and collaboration gave place to controversy, their disagreements are in themselves illuminating. One can understand Keynes and the neo-Keynesians better if one is also familiar with what Robertson had to say. Thus John Hicks once observed that the effect on his own mind, and on Nicholas Kaldor's, of the *General Theory* had been profound. But, he went on, 'we have each of us been led, sometimes consciously, sometimes unconsciously, through Keynes to Robertson'.[4] The fact remains that whereas Keynes's contribution, even when criticised, is everywhere accorded a position of central importance, Robertson's contribution is almost wholly ignored. Although it would be wrong to claim parity of treatment, the disparity is too vast to be justified.

35

Apart from any concern about unfairness of treatment, there is another reason for looking back at Robertsonian economics. With regard both to diagnosis and policy, he may be said to stand somewhere between Keynesianism and monetarism, and the views of those who occupy such intermediate positions may deserve closer attention than they were wont to receive when the battle between the two schools was at its noisy height. To say this is not, of course, to suggest that anything would be gained by a blurring of issues in a search for weak-minded compromise – something that Robertson himself never sought in his controversy with Keynes before the war or with the neo-Keynesians after the war. It would be no tribute to him to try to do so today.

Of the various points raised in that controversy the one most immediately relevant was Robertson's insistence on the importance of changes in the money supply and his emphasis on the continuing need for control. The triumph of the Keynesian Revolution was to lead to the degradation of money and to its being assigned the role of a docile slave working quietly and largely unnoticed in the service of its fiscal masters. Robertson was one of the few economists in postwar Britain to protest strongly about this development and to this extent might be called a monetarist. But it is one thing to stress the importance of controlling the money supply and a different matter to accept the full range of ideas held to be central to monetarist doctrine. Admittedly monetarism is not a precisely specified creed, but Robertson would appear, nevertheless, to have been too heretical for posthumous membership of the sect. For he did not believe that the private economy was inherently stable, that disturbances when they occurred would be quickly dealt with by rapidly clearing markets, that structural matters could be largely ignored, and that changes in velocity were of minor importance. His emphasis was rather on dynamic change, on equilibrium positions that were always shifting before they could be attained, on the ignorance of all the actors, and on errors of forecasting in a world of Knightian uncertainty. The point can be made succinctly by saying that Robertson was a 'non-Walrasian monetarist'. The picture thus conveyed may slightly distort both Robertson and Walras but, as a rough likeness, it will serve.

Of course, it is necessary to add that the label of 'non-Walrasian monetarist' could be applied to others as well as to Robertson. In a well-known paper, Franco Modigliani has made the point as follows: 'Milton Friedman was once quoted as saying, "We are all Keynesians, now," and I am quite prepared to reciprocate that "We are all monetarists" – if by monetarism is meant assigning to the stock of money a major role in determining output and prices'.[5] The real dispute, he went on to say, concerns the need for stabilisation policies and the form they should take. Admittedly this remark might not be fully endorsed by all the leading British Keynesians, and we should not, in any case, expect to find any close uniformity of views among 'non-Walrasian monetarists' – for example, with regard to income policies. The point to be made here is that, with views of this kind now receiving more attention, there is a case for looking back at those held by some of the great economists of an earlier generation. Robertson's views are of particular relevance in this respect.

It would be a hopeless undertaking to attempt, within the compass of a single chapter, to provide a comprehensive survey of Robertsonian economics together with detailed comparative references to the many aspects of monetarism and Keynesianism respectively. Attention must obviously be confined to a selection of the main issues. Even within these limitations, the task is made more difficult by the fact that Robertson wrote no 'General Theory' and, as we have observed, his somewhat scattered contributions are not at all well-known today. It is helpful, therefore, that we now have at hand John Presley's guide to his writings including his controversy with Keynes. Moreover, Donald Moggridge's great edition of the *Collected Writings of John Maynard Keynes* affords helpful insights by making available various papers that throw additional light both on the early partnership between Keynes and Robertson and on the reasons for its collapse with consequences which, in my view, were to prove damaging to both of them.

II

In his first book, *A Study of Industrial Fluctuations*, [6] Robertson set out to investigate the causes of fluctuations in real output and employment as well as in prices. Various explanations were examined, including variations in harvests, but the one that was to remain as a theme through all his subsequent work was the instability of the inducement to invest. This instability reflected such factors as technological change, the aging of the capital stock, its durability, and its indivisibility; and the fluctuations were magnified by errors of forecasting over what were often lengthy gestation periods. In this respect, his explanation was obviously similar to Joseph Schumpeter's, although we are told by Presley that he knew nothing of Schumpeter's work until 1927.[7] The psychological factor – later to be much stressed by A. C. Pigou[8] and subsequently revived and again over-emphasised as the theory of 'animal spirits' – could aggravate this instability but was not its basic cause. Nor was Robertson prepared to accept Ralph G. Hawtrey's view that the explanation was to be found in changes in monetary policy.[9] Later, in *Banking Policy and the Price Level*, he again rejected Hawtrey's view that 'the trade cycle is a purely monetary phenomenon'.[10] The point was driven home by constructing models of a non-monetary economy that was characterised by unanticipated, or inadequately anticipated, changes in the real variables. It might be objected today that if the real cycle followed a regular course, it would become 'rationally anticipated'. Although Robertson perceived some such regularity, he was inclined to stress the individuality of every cycle and never subscribed to regularity of timing to the extent that Schumpeter was to do in *Business Cycles*.[11]

Instability, in his view, was to be regarded as the price of progress and this price, in terms of adjustments of work effort in response to changes in the marginal efficiency of investment, might be accepted voluntarily in an economy with cooperative management. With separation of management from labour, the trade-off between progress and stability would, however, be biased in favour of the former because preferences differed, and the social harm would be further increased if the required decline in work were concentrated on some of the workers in the form of unemployment.[12] This discussion of a trade-off between work and leisure can now be looked at afresh with the modern analysis of Robert E. Lucas, Jr, and Leonard A. Rapping in mind.[13]

These models deserve mention because they show so clearly that Robertson regarded the private economy as inherently unstable. In his list of the characteristics of monetarism, Thomas Mayer includes, as one would expect, a belief 'in the inherent stability of the private sector'.[14] Douglas D. Purvis makes the same point by saying that, in monetarist theory: 'The real rate of interest is (approximately) a constant'.[15] How important is this difference of views about the economic system? The market, if allowed to operate, will bring about structural adjustments. There would be no conflict of opinion between Robertson and the monetarists on that score, but there would remain a difference about the speed and ease of adjustment. In a non-Walrasian world these frictional problems can be serious, as monetarist would no doubt agree. As this is so, it will not do to proceed as though the world were in fact Walrasian. Moreover, Robertson was not considering, at this point, the transfer of resources from declining to expanding industries but rather the cyclical instability of the sector producing durable goods, which would be re-flected in cyclical-structural unemployment – or, in monetarist ter-minology, in cyclical fluctuations in the 'natural rate of unemployment'. It could still be argued that the workers in these industries were aware of the industries' instability and, as they had chosen to accept such jobs, the periodic spells of unemployment could be regarded as 'volun-tary'. Robertson, whose starting-point in the *Study* was history, not abstract analysis, was deeply conscious of limited opportunities and errors of foresight, and thus felt impelled to recommend counter-cyclical fluctuations in public investment – long before 'Kenyesian' fiscal policy has been mooted. He also suggested that steps could be taken to im-prove the information available to managers about the intentions of other firms – a hint at 'indicative planning', although the aim was not, as he explained many years later,[16] to stimulate investment for the sake of growth but rather to restrain excesses. One could put Robertson's point by saying that certain industries have peak-load problems, which arise every few years. If this problem could be eased by counter-cyclical public investment or by improving the supply of information, resources could be used more effectively and at less social cost. Whether this aim could really be achieved in practice by such means is, of course, a question that requires evidence of a kind that was not at the disposal of the young Robertson.

It may be held that, for a variety of reasons concerned with changes in industrial organisation, innovational investment is no longer so unstable as Robertson and Schumpeter once believed. This is an empirical matter. A good deal of empirical evidence would also be required to give satisfactory meaning – quantitative meaning – to the 'inherent stability' attributed by monetarists to the private economy. In other words, the neglect of structural problems and allocational detail[17] in monetarism cannot simply be assumed to be appropriate. To quote from Lucas and Rapping: 'To define what is meant by reasonable stability, and to discover how expectations are revised when such stability ceases to obtain, seem to us to be a crucial, unresolved problem'.[18]

What cannot be in doubt, however, is that much more serious problems arise when instability spreads throughout the whole economy, affecting the consumption goods industries with feedback, by means of the accelerator, to the investment goods industries. It was this transmission mechanism that could lead to inflationary booms followed by slumps and thus to 'a purposeless and obscene orgy of destruction'.[19] Much of Robertson's subsequent work was devoted to an analysis of the transmission mechanism, but before passing on to that particular topic, it is necessary to consider whether, with attention now directed to a money economy, the real sector will have been superseded by the money supply as the principal *initiator* of instability. What importance then is to be attached to (a) fluctuations in the marginal efficiency of investment as compared to (b) changes in the rate of growth of the money supply, as the match that lights the fuse? Robertson's reading of economic history led him to believe that (a) was the right answer. Monetarists come down in favour of (b), but there are differences of emphasis between different members of that school. Thus Milton Friedman and Anna J. Schwartz did not accord much attention to the 'real' factors as the initiators of instability in their statistical and historical work on the United States economy.[20] For example, such factors as the weakening demand for housing and for new automobiles, which had featured so prominently in earlier explanations of the 1929 downturn, received little attention. There is also a revealing passage in another of Friedman's papers where he refers to Wicksell's theory of the natural rate of interest and goes on to say: 'The monetary authority can make the market rate less than the natural rate only by inflation. It can make the market rate higher than the natural rate only by deflation'.[21] Friedman's attention appears to be directed to changes in the *market* rate, whereas

Wicksell's own emphasis had been mainly on changes in the *natural* rate with a market rate that 'does not adapt itself quickly enough to these changes'.[22] This was also Robertson's emphasis.

It is hard to see why a belief in the inherent stability of the private sector should be pushed to the point of neglecting the effect of changes in investment demand in initiating instability. After all, the monetary authorities may be prepared to accommodate changes in the demand for public finance, although they are not, admittedly, under quite the same political compulsion to do so. Such neglect does not seem a necessary component of monetarism. Perhaps it is not so regarded – not at least by all monetarists,

David Laidler, for his part, seems to accord what, by Purvis's standard, is a non-monetarist role to the natural state. Thus he writes that the monetarist

> view of the stability of the private sector is quite compatible with the Keynesian hypothesis about the relative instability of the marginal efficiency of investment – here perhaps I disagree with Mayer – for what is required for stability in the private sector when the money supply is following a steady growth path is that demand for money function be sufficiently stable and sufficiently interest inelastic for fluctuations in the marginal efficiency of investment to result in interest rate fluctuations rather than in disturbances to output and employment, not that the marginal efficiency of investment schedule remain stable.[23]

There would appear, however, to be a difference of emphasis between Laidler's position and that of Karl Brunner and Allan Meltzer: 'Our proposition asserts that cyclical instability is mainly the product of government policies that are imposed on a stabilising private sector'.[24] Admittedly the word 'mainly' in the quotation may be important, especially when allowance is made for the immense growth in public expenditure relative to GNP and to industrial investment since Robertson's early work appeared. In his later work he too laid heavy stress on the destabilizing effects of government policies without, however, abandoning his earlier belief in the importance of a fluctuating demand for new capital.

It is important to note that, even if the inadequately anticipated changes were often to *originate* in the private sector, this would not be inconsistent with the monetarist view that changes in the money supply are the main cause of magnified changes in the total of money income. That is a different point. How valid it is depends (i) upon the size of the secondary expansion or contraction relative to the initial change in investment and (ii) upon what is happening to the velocity of circulation – as Laidler implies in the quotation above.

If the private economy is 'inherently stable', this stability should extend to the demand for money, and monetarists claim to have established, as a fact, that this is so – or reasonably close to being so, although long-term trend adjustments may occur. Robertson, for his part, laid great stress on unstable velocity, but there are different issues to be disentangled here. Stability of demand relative to what? Robertson was stressing the instability of the demand for money relative to income – current income. The arguments that actually determine what the demand for money will be are, however, a different matter, for 'it is not necessary to suppose that he [some person] is arriving at decisions about the size of his money stock solely by reference to the size of his income – he may be considering also the size of his total wealth or his total annual turnover. But, however *arrived at*, it can be *expressed* as a proportion of income'.[25] Like Friedman, he could have included permanent income as an argument without affecting his conclusion. But it was K – the inverse of the velocity of circulation – that was 'the Prince of Denmark in the Hamlet of the Cambridge Equation'.[26]

Some of Robertson's remarks – for example about 'the incalculable K' – seem to imply scepticism about the possibility of finding any stable demand function for money.[27] The 'incalculable K' might then be ponderously translated to mean, not that it is a mere 'will-o'-the-wisp', but rather that no function with a manageable number of quantifiable arguments is likely to be discovered. It must be conceded that, if this is what he meant, he was only expressing a hunch; for he was not in a position to embark upon a detailed empirical investigation – no computer, no team of research assistants, virtually no secretarial assistance.

The crucial point for short-term stabilisation policy is, however, that a stable demand function for money containing several arguments is quite consistent with a volatile income velocity – as Friedman himself has conceded.[28] This would seem to warrant the placing of emphasis on changes in *MV* rather than simply in *M*. Of course, it is always open to monetarists to object that they are not concerned with short-term instability or that they are sceptical about the effectiveness of short-run discretionary policies. The fact remains that Friedman and Schwartz did not regard the slump of 1929–33 as covering too short a period to be worth studying, and they did lay great stress – and rightly so – on the fall in the money stock in the United States. If, however, changes in *M* over this period deserve consideration, so do changes in *V*, and these were large. Over the critical first year, 1930, compared with 1929, velocity fell by 13 per cent, while the money stock fell by 2 per cent; between 1929 and 1933, both fell by about the same, 30 per cent. There is no need to claim that changes in the rate of growth of the money supply and in velocity are quite independent; but there is also no need to assume that the latter is simply dependent upon the former.[29]

III

In *Money*[30] and in *Banking*, Robertson devoted more attention to the transmission of instability through the financial mechanism than he had done in the *Study*. Decisions to save and to invest were not taken by the same people, or not entirely so, and it was not to be expected that differences would be so reconciled by the banks and the financial markets as to ensure a stable level of total expenditure or, in a growing economy, a changing level of expenditure appropriate to the rate of growth. At this time he was working closely with Keynes and was probably taking the lead in analysing the effect of changes in the money supply and its velocity. Keynes observed: 'I like this latest version [of *Banking*], though God knows it is concise'.[31] (It was not only concise but marred by an idiosyncratic terminology, which no one else ever adopted.) Keynes expressed his particular admiration for chapter 5 ' – most new and important. I think it is substantially right and at last I have no material criticism'.[32] In this chapter, which followed a discussion of the instability of investment, Robertson was, in effect, explaining how a divergence between intended saving and investment would be followed by adjustments in unplanned saving which, as we would now say, would achieve *ex post* equality. His elaboration of the distinction between voluntary and forced saving included a hybrid, which he described as 'induced lacking'. This occurred when a change in prices caused by a change in the money supply or in its velocity changed real balances so that people were induced to alter their expenditure in order to restore, or partially restore, their real balances. In the opposite circumstances they would spend more. That is to say, changes in real balances would effect total expenditure directly, not just indirectly through the effect of the rate of interest on investment. Thus what has come to be called the Pigou effect[33] could also be called the Robertson effect – or, indeed, the Keynes effect, for Robertson explains that he derived this concept from Keynes himself![34]

The evolution of Robertson's ideas by the mid-thirties can be seen in his 1934 *Economic Journal* article. 'Industrial Fluctuation and the Natural Rate of Interest'. He had naturally been much influenced both by Keynes's *Treatise on Money* (1930) and by seeing drafts of the *General Theory*, although he did not agree fully with either of these works. Whereas Keynes abandoned and condemned the concept of a natural rate of interest, Robertson continued to use it. He did not, however, confine his attention to full employment, as did Wicksell. There are, on the contrary, whole series of 'natural rates' – or expenditure-stabilising rates – corresponding to different levels of output. His starting-point is the middle of the cycle when a rise in the marginal efficiency of investment occurs and raises the natural rate corresponding to that level of output. If the market rate is not then raised correspondingly in order to discourage investment and encourage saving, there will be a net rise in total expenditure. During the gestation period before output can respond, prices will rise in what is implicitly assumed to be 'forced saving' in the sense that some people are holding larger balances than they wish to hold, so that – to use terminology that Robertson did not employ – the necessary *ex post* equality of savings with investment need not happen to coincide with an equilibrium position. There will, however, be some shift to profits, which will raise the propensity to save *voluntarily* at any given level of income. We may note, in passing, the obvious link between Robertson's theory and the growth theory developed by Kaldor after the war (1955–6) in which distributional changes raise profits and savings when investment demand is high and lower than when it is low, thus reducing the long-term instability of the economy.

Robertson was cautious. Wages would be pushed up in turn, and prices would rise yet again. There was a further complication discussed in his *Lectures*, which were largely composed long before their publication (1957–9). What matters is not so much the propensity to *save* but the propensity to spend – to *spend* on capital goods as well as on consumption goods. Increased business savings could not therefore be regarded as simply a leakage if, as a result, investment plans were also increased. (His reminder that an 'increase in saving may generate an increase in capital outlay'[35] was, in effect, to be taken up much later by the New Cambridge School.)

The continuing boom could be ended by the banking system restricting the supply of new money but, even if this did not happen, it would end with the increased flow of output after the gestation period and a decline in the marginal efficiency of investment. An interesting inference may be drawn at this point. Although the private economy is unstable and its instability may be seriously magnified by an elastic supply of funds, an indefinitely prolonged inflation would not result. Indefinite inflation in a closed economy requires a public deficit financed by monetary expansion. (In an open economy with fixed exchange rates, it can continue for a longer period if the country in question is inflating less than the rest of the world. How long will depend upon the country's importance in international trade, on the size of the reserves held elsewhere, and upon capital flows.)

In the article mentioned above, Robertson passed over the effect of changes in real income on voluntary savings, as distinct from changes in its distribution. This omission was made good in a 1936 article 'Effective Demand and the Multiplier'.[36] It is true that this was a critical article. He was sceptical about the stability of the marginal propensity to consume, and he held (very strongly) that more attention should be paid to the feed-back to investment demand through the accelerator. ('Dogs wag tails, as well as tails dogs.') The fact remains that, if the two articles are taken together, Robertson had developed a model of the cycle that anticipated in many respects the Keynesian models subsequently developed by Michal Kalecki[37] and Kaldor.[38] Keynes, himself, it will be recalled, did not produce any model of this kind.

This was, however, the time when differences of opinion between Robertson and the Keynesians became acute.[39] These differences related not so much to the instability of industrial investment as to the transmission process. First, there was the confusion caused by the two senses in which Keynes used the terms 'savings' and 'investment'. If 'savings and investment are the same thing',[40] no change in real income is needed to make them equal – just as no profound biological forces are required to make an elephant's trunk equal to its proboscis![41] On this basis there would be no role for the multiplier, the theory of liquidity preference, etc. – in fact, no transmission mechanism at all.

The second disputed point was the Keynesian contention that a rise in investment will finance itself, which confused two separate issues: (i) the effect of a change in real income on voluntary saving and (ii) the financial requirements for a net change in expenditure. Robertson very properly pointed out that the rise in income could not occur without a rise in real expenditure. Keynes subsequently went some way to meet this point by introducing the concept of 'finance'; but it was only a grudging concession and one so confusingly expressed that Robertson remained unsatisfied.[42] The other explanation, which was to become the standard one in so many Keynesian textbooks, was that rising investment would raise income, and that the consequential increase in the demand for working balances could raise the rate of interest. But it was still necessary to explain how expenditure, and therefore income, could increase in the first place. This could occur only if there was some elasticity in the supply of funds, and unless this elasticity was perfect, changes in investment or in saving would have a *direct* effect on the rate of interest – a point that Keynes vehemently denied. To express Robertson's point by reference to the IS/LM construction of which he disapproved,[43] a shift in the *IS* curve is bound to affect the rate of interest unless *LM* is horizontal. It is to be hoped that the recent controversy about crowding-out has at least dispelled any lingering Keynesian confusion over this issue.

The third point was the determination of the rate of interest. At an early stage in the debate, Hicks sought to demonstrate that there is no inconsistency between the liquidity preference theory and the loanable funds approach.[44] But the latter fell out of popular favour and remains under a cloud in the United Kingdom even today. Indeed it is not uncommon for students to suppose that the loanable funds theory can be identified with the proposition that the rate of interest is determined solely by savings and investment! As we have observed, however, it was an essential part of Robertson's theory, from *Money* and *Banking* onwards, that the flow of investible funds would be partly determined by injections or withdrawals that reflected changes in the supply of money and in the demand for money balances. The liquidity preference theory, which attempted to explain why velocity changed, could therefore become one constituent part of the more comprehensive loanable funds theory. Robertson, for his part, was at pains to list the various reasons for injections and withdrawals, and this was surely an illuminating approach.[45]

The issue in dispute here was related to the Keynesian claim that liquidity preference, given the supply of money, provided an explanation of why there *is* a rate of interest at all. For it will not do to claim that the rate of interest is simply based on expectations about the future of the level of the rate of interest! On this issue Robertson was not, of course, alone in his criticism. Hicks observed that Keynes had left the rate 'hanging by its own bootstraps', and this point was also recognised by Kaldor and Kelecki. All three tried to find a solution by saying that the bond rate was based on expected short-term rates plus a risk premium. Robertson, for his part, was not prepared to admit that interest had no better parentage than the fiat of the monetary authorities.

It is perfectly sensible to maintain that productivity and thrift explain why interest occurs at all, although the *actual* levels of rates for loans of various kinds will depend at any time partly upon other factors as well. Robertson went a step further however, when he asserted – in true Ricardian style – that saving and investments are the dominant factors in the long run. Why is not the long run a succession of short runs, in every one of which the other forces may be important? Moreover, even if there are occasions when the money stock is not changing and its velocity is steady, so that productivity and thrift are the determining factors, this position of stability may be reached at *different* levels of income – as had been recognised by Robertson himself when he used different natural rates in his 1934 article. We are coming back here to the question whether changes in monetary expenditure can alter the real quantities more than briefly. We shall return to this point below (pp. 48–52).

This section may be concluded by observing that Robertson was highly sceptical about the existence of a 'liquidity trap' and pointed out that Keynes himself had confessed to being unaware of any historical example.[46] He complained that 'a theory of money which insists on working everything through the bond market – a College Bursar's theory as it has been called – is lacking in realism and comprehensiveness'.[47] Not only must equities be taken into account but *also* the direct effect on purchases of changes in the supply of money – purchases of capital goods and of consumer's goods as well. Thus he returned to the Pigou effect which, as we have seen, was the Keynes-Robertson effect of an earlier date.

IV

Before we attempt to consider the arguments for or against the various policies recommended for stabilisation, we must face a basic objection expressed as follows by Frank H. Hahn:[48] 'The monetarists in some sense do not just object to Keynesian' – or, we may insert, to Robertsonian – 'remedies; they argue that there are no Keynesian ills to remedy.' He goes on to say: 'The main conclusion is not only that money does not matter unless its stock is changed randomly, but also that inflation resulting from a systematic monetary policy does not matter. This, paradoxical as it may sound, is the strict monetarist view'.[49]

Hahn is concerned in particular with the strict view of the new monetarist wing, the rational expectations wing.[50] It is obviously impossible here to attempt to an even remotely adequate assessment of this highly sophisticated analysis, which can be too easily caricatured. The emphasis placed on private reactions to public policies is undoubtedly important but, in what is perhaps a rather Philistine way, one suspects that it has been overdone. Private people devote only limited attention to these policies, and this is not a wholly irrational attitude, for Adam Smith's division of labour surely applies. A kind of natural selection may then sort out the unfit, but this will take time and policies will change again so that some of the unfit may even be reprieved. Moreover, it is one thing to foresee a change in the *direction* of policy and another matter to give it an accurate *quantitative dimension*.

Finally, it need not be assumed that private reactions will always frustrate public policies.

It has been pointed out by Thomas M. Humphrey[51] that Robertson himself had developed a theory of rational expectations with regard to the foreign-exchange market, which he put forward as early as 1928 in the second edition of *Money*. There was, however, no question of his anticipating this theory in its more general application, for Robertson was not assuming a world in which all markets are quickly cleared. The point can be put by saying that he was assuming 'market failure' over a large part of the economy. It may be permissible to observe in passing that the term 'market failure' is an unfortunate one, which may be taken to imply some basic flaw in the price system which, if it cannot be removed, would warrant the abandonment of the system itself. That, of course, is not what monetarists intend, nor is it an inference that Robertson himself would have accepted. But ill-chosen terms can be unintentionally persuasive. Apart from any such confusion, we need not in my view endorse without question the assumption that a Walrasian price system would, in all respects, be superior to one where some markets do not clear at once. We may add here that it is a common error to suppose that administered prices preclude price competition, for price competition may be expressed in different ways according to the market structure. In Robertson's words: 'nobody doubts that the sellers of goods normally quote a price instead of putting their goods up to auction; the question is how much freedom they have in deciding what price to quote'.[52] Thus he avoided the common non-Walrasian error of supposing that when prices are administered, profit margins have no better basis than custom or convention. The basic point, however, it that we do not live in a Walrasian world and Robertson's policy recommendations were based, in effect, on the acceptance of this fact of life.

In deciding whether a change in monetary expenditure (positive or negative) would change the real quantities, in determining what change would seem appropriate, and in choosing the methods, fiscal or monetary or both by which this change might best be effected, it is crucially important to specify the starting point. Is unemployment at its 'natural rate' so that the problem is to ensure steady progress? Or is the economy suffering from severe inflation or deflation, so that the task is to get it back to stability? Today we are preoccupied with the problem of coping with a heritage of inflationary policies and, as we have good cause to know, the transition to stability is not a smooth and easy path. During the interwar period, Robertson and Keynes were, of course, concerned with the problems of deflation and heavy unemployment. But it could be held – and was held by some people – that even in the early thirties unemployment was 'voluntary' in the sense that cuts in money wages would remedy the position. It was Keynes, who had already begun to correspond with Robertson in 1933[53] about Pigou's *Theory of Unemployment*,[54] who dealt with the argument that unemployment was to be explained by the fact that the labour market did not clear.[55] Two of the several points made are of particular relevance and constitute, in my view, important problems for the modern theory of rational expectations.

(1)   Even if there were some mechanism by which a general cut in money wages could be quickly achieved – thus avoiding the harmful effect on expectations of a sagging wage level – it did not follow that real wages would be reduced. For demand in a closed economy would then fall, and prices would also decline in proportion – precisely in those circumstances where the product markets cleared with Walrasian promptitude. There would therefore be no way in which the workers themselves could bring about a fall in real wages. Consider, at this point, the contention that only unexpected changes in effective demand affect the position – a contention put forward in a recent paper on unemployment in Britain in the early thirties.[56] Presumably the argument is that, if workers in 1929 had foreseen the impending fall in effective demand, they would have settled for lower wages. Had they done so, however, effective demand would have been still lower. In short, we are in danger of being caught up in circular reasoning – unless the real balance effect is instantaneous.

Kalecki discussed a situation where prices were administered and did not fall.[57] Real wages would then decline, but so would employment unless the non-wage sector were induced by the change in money wages to raise its *real* expenditure.

(2)   With no mechanism for bringing about a quick general cut in money wages, each group of workers is obliged to consider its *relative* position.[58] In short, the unions are caught in a Prisoner's Dilemma. I must confess I do not know how the rational expectations school would deal with the problem of the Prisoner's Dilemma, which raises difficult

analytical issues, for the reaction functions can no longer be assumed to be independent.

It followed from Keynes's reasoning that the only beneficial effect from a cut in money wages would be a rise in real balances. But this could be achieved more easily by direct action to raise the money stock. Thus a case was established for discretionary action, and we may add that, in the depths of a depression, this case was not weakened by quite the same problems of forecasting and implementations that plague a policy of fine-tuning.

If, then, monetary expenditure needed to be increased, how could this best be done? Keynesian policy is nowadays taken to mean fiscal policy, but the emphasis in the *Treatise on Money*[59] was on monetary policy. It was Robertson who was then the sceptic. The long-term rate could not be pushed down so quickly as Keynes believed and, in any case, the interest-elasticity of investment demand was low. As Presley has reminded us, Robertson was not prepared to place much faith on monetary policy alone in the evidence he submitted to the Macmillan Committee.[60] Indeed this scepticism was so strong as to lend support to William Fellner's observation that there is 'a stagnationist corner' in Robertsonian theory[61] – at least so far as monetary policy alone is concerned. At this stage he was placing little faith in the real-balance effect alone, even if brought into play by an active policy of increasing the amount of money in people's pockets. It would, however, be inconsistent with what he had said earlier, and was to repeat later, to infer that he expected the inducement to invest to remain indefinitely at a low level. It would not, and in this sense the private economy was stabilising. The point was rather that recovery from the misery of depression could be speeded up by appropriate policies.

In recommending fiscal policy, Robertson's main emphasis was still on counter-cyclical public investment, and it should be recorded that this was the weapon on which Keynes placed most faith as late as the 1940s, when the British *White Paper on Employment Policy* was being drafted. As the *Collected Writings* (Volume 27) reveals, Keynes was apprehensive about a policy for changing taxation, apart from variations in social security contributions. Experience was to show, however, that he and Robertson exaggerated what could be done by public investment. Robertson, in his *Lectures*[62] did not oppose tax cuts, and later recommended to the Canadian Royal Commission on Banking and Finance that these might be speeded up.[63] He was particularly attracted to built-in stabilisers and – with some qualifications – to buffer stocks. He was, of course, well aware of the difficulties of fine-tuning. Moreover, his aim was not complete stability, even if attainable. Some instability was the price of progress, though that price could be reduced.

Philip Cagan has observed that 'Indeed, a monetarist in good standing need not oppose all discretionary monetary policy'.[64] It is in place to add that a number of economists who would not be described as 'Keynesian' – for example, Pigou himself and Gottfried Haberler – were prepared to extend discretionary action in order to include fiscal policy when an economy had been allowed to fall into deep depression.

V

If, then, expenditure is to be increased, is a rise in prices to be anticipated? If it should occur, is it reasonable to hope to achieve a low non-accelerating inflation rate of unemployment (NAIRU)? For, if inflation should accelerate, then the gains to be achieved from a rise in expenditure would be short-lived, as Friedman has repeatedly emphasised.

As we have observed, Robertson postulated rising prices in his pre-war work because time would be required before output could be raised. He placed less emphasis than Hawtrey did on the effect of reductions in stocks[65] because, although he paid a great deal of attention to stocks, he was preoccupied at this point with changes in work-in-progress rather than with inventories of finished goods. Thus he was assuming a *flexprice* model in the product market. Subsequently, after the gestation period, there would be a flood of output which, together with weakening demand for capital goods, would lead to a downturn.

In his reappraisal of Keynesian economics, Hicks had laid heavy emphasis on the distinction between *fixprice* and *flexprice* models, which reflect differences in the ways in which prices are fixed.[66] Robertson had taken this into account in his *Lectures*.[67] We must, however, be careful here. Even in a model where prices are administered and profit margins really are constant, prices may be forced upwards by increases in wages, which are not inflexible *upwards* even if – in the United States more than the United Kingdom – contracts may have some effect in delaying the response.

The slope of the marginal cost curves becomes crucially important as we look farther ahead. Keynes made the usual classical assumption that they would be rising, but was to be quickly challenged by John T. Dunlop[68] and Kalecki.[69] Keynes was then to modify this assumption.[70] It is true that constant productivity in manufacturing and the services industries will not suffice to produce constant prices, for there will still be a substantial *flexprice* primary product sector and, moreover, with lack of homogeneity in the labour force, rising wages in some jobs will not be offset by falling wages elsewhere. If, however, productivity is actually rising, then it is conceivable that there may be a range of output over which the price level will be fairly steady, and belief in such a range became deeply embedded in Keynesian thought. Whether this is realistic or not depends upon the relative weights of all of these different considerations and not, except in the very short run, upon the existence of administered prices.

At this point we need to distinguish between two different meanings of the 'natural rate of unemployment'. First there is the frictional minimum – which we can designate UN_1 – corresponding to what used to be called full employment. Secondly, there is the level of unemployment at which inflationary expectations will be realised – UN_2. In a situation where UN_1 and UN_2 coincide, attempts to trade inflation for more employment will fail. If, however, unemployment is well above UN_1, it is possible for expansion to proceed without rising prices and, over a range of employment, UN_2 will have no unique value.[71] The natural rate of interest will also have no unique value. This situation could be represented by a simple Phillips curve, with changes in prices on the Y-axis, which does not only become flatter to the right but actually becomes asymptotic – until unemployment is so heavy as to break the money-wage ratchet. Monetarists neglect this possibility by assuming that if UN_2 is attained, UN_1 will be also. Without discretionary action to raise expenditure, however, this coincidence would require indefinite flexibility in money wages and a fast-working real-balance effect.

If it should be the case that there is such a range of output, how do we interpret Robertson's remark that in the long run, the rate of interest would be determined by savings and investment? It is true, of course, that in this theory the economy would not be stuck indefinitely at some point within this range, for the marginal efficiency of investment was always changing, so that the economy would be constantly moving from one position to another. He himself identified *the* natural rate as that corresponding to a mid-point in the cycle – a statistical average.[72] If, however, the range of fluctuation could be reduced, as he believed, by policy, then a different average would presumably emerge. A similar question is raised by Hicks's second essay on Keynes and the Classics.[73] In his model there is the same range of output over which prices are constant but with prices rising and real balanes falling when unemployment is very low and prices falling and real balances rising when unemployment is high enough to break the money-wage ratchet. Again there is no unique position where the classical forces dominate, but rather there is a set of limits to the range over which they do not dominate. It is a range within which changes in monetary expenditure can change the real quantities, as Hicks, of course, implied.

Empirically there may, in fact, be no such range of steady prices with rising output. The old cycle was, after all, a cycle of prices as well as production. A. J. Brown has drawn attention to the fact that prices before the war began to rise from a low point on the cycle[74] and a recent backward glance at Brown's work has confirmed G. D. N. Worswick in his belief that a permanent incomes policy is highly desirable.[75] It is an inference that does not follow logically, for an incomes policy may not be acceptable or may not be workable without incurring heavy costs in other directions. The fact remains that we should face a difficult problem if increases in output even from low cyclical levels were to lead to rising prices, which then generated accelerating inflation which, in turn, could only be ended by miserable periods of stagflation. This would be a worse situation – much worse – than that usually envisaged by Friedman, who assumes that unemployment will tend towards its natural rate, in the sense of UN_1, and then directs his attention to the consequence of trying to push it down to still lower levels. Fortunately we need not generalise on the basis of interwar experience when the increases in prices and wages during an upswing were restoring the declines that had occurred during the downswing, as Robertson pointed out[76] in commenting on

Brown's statistics. For, from a historical perspective, the money-wage ratchet is a comparatively modern phenomenon. In short there was no need to suppose that the upswing of the older cycle would necessarily lead to accelerating inflation if the monetary authorities exercised reasonable restraint. If such acceleration could be avoided, then once more changes in expenditure could alter the real quantities.

It is a different matter if wages do not fall during a decline in activity, for an inflationary trend may then become established. Robertson was much exercised by this danger, and his concern was expressed in the First Report of the Council on Prices, Productivity and Incomes.[77] The need to prevent rising prices and wages in good years then became crucially important. Might NAIRU not yet be attainable at some positive rate of increase in prices? Fellner doubts whether any rate above zero will carry conviction.[78] and I am inclined to agree.[79] Robertson, for his part, came down firmly against rising prices.

Robertson devoted much thought to an incomes policy as a means of achieving this end. It need scarcely be said that he had no sympathy for the view, which he attributed to Kaldor, that incomes policy alone would do the trick.[80] Given such financial restraint, however, would an incomes policy help? He was strongly opposed to the use of controls, which were inefficient and restricted freedom. He did not, however, share Friedman's view that trade-union policy was irrelevant to inflation. The process of checking inflation could not be achieved without a shock and a jolt. 'How great that shock and jolt need be, and in particular how largely it takes the form of unemployment *would* depend largely on the wage policy of Trade Unions; and that is where good leadership from inside, and even ear-stroking from outside, would have a genuine part to play'.[81] 'Ear-stroking' was his somewhat whimsical expression for the joint discussion of such matters as general guide-lines. For the labour market is not a market where we can simply think of individuals putting forward their demands and embarking upon job-search in an individualistic way. It is substantially a market of labour monopolies and the leaders of every union, even if sensible and well-intentioned, must guess at what guidelines to take to protect their relative positions. In this Prisoner's Dilemma situation, it is just possible that some discussion of an appropriate guideline might help. There was no question, however, of his recommending the detailed official control of the labour market. It is true that he favoured reform of the system of national collective bargaining, but that was, of course, a different matter.[82]

It is one thing to foster recovery from a deep depression, but a different matter to devise policies that will keep an economy growing at a high level of employment without accelerating inflation. In the seventies and eighties that may seem a remotely academic problem, but it was not so in the period after the immediate postwar difficulties were over. Employment was at a high level, but the rise in prices in the United States was very modest in the fifties and sixties and it looked as though a situation similar to the New Era (1923–9) might have been reached. In Britain the strain on the balance of payments as well as the rise in prices must be taken into account but, even so, inflation was not severe. What was important was not to press unemployment down to an unsustainably low level, but these, unfortunately, were the years when the theory of a trade-off between inflation and unemployment were in fashion. When the Council on Prices, Productivity and Incomes suggested that unemployment rather above the current level of 1.9 per cent would be appropriate, it was vilified for saying so. It is ironic to reflect that Keynes himself had said in *The Times* in 1937 that 'We are more in need today of a rightly distributed demand than of a greater aggregate demand'.[83] Unemployment was then about 9 per cent on the modern basis of reckoning – rather more than the level in Britain in 1980! Keynes drew Robertson's attention to these (then forthcoming) articles[84] and observed that his views on current policy did not differ greatly from those expressed by Robertson at Harvard in 1936.[85]

If Keynes was cautious – surely overcautious – in his assessment of the level to which unemployment could be reduced by increasing expenditure, he was intransigent in his opposition to dear money which, even in a boom, was to be avoided 'as we would hell-fire'. For demand might fall again and: 'A low enough rate of interest cannot be achieved if we allow it to be believed that better terms will be obtainable from time to time by those who keep their resources liquid'.[86] After the war a low range of interest rates became the target, with the money supply the accommodating variable and, at the same time, Keynes's caution about the safe level of unemployment was forgotten.

It seems strange that Keynes should have displayed so great a lack of practical judgement in ignoring the far greater danger that 'madmen in authority who hear voices in the air' would hear those voices say that the money supply is unimportant, with the agreeable corollary that the public debt can be financed on easy terms.[87] It is true that this was a delusion – but madmen have delusions. As Robertson pointed out: 'if Governments do not see fit to pay rather higher interest rates because capital is scarce they may easily find themselves having to pay much higher rates in a desperate attempt to keep pace with the foreseen depreciation of money'.[88] Thus the policy would not achieve its fiscal ends, just as the attempts to reduce unemployment to very low levels at the cost of inflation was doomed to fail.

One can only reflect with sadness about what might have happened if the old Keynes-Robertson axis had not broken in the thirties and control of the money supply had been part of Keynesian policy. The Keynesian Revolution would then have been less violent, but it might have been more enduring.

NOTES

1.   The author is indebted for comments on an earlier draft to William Fellner, John Hicks, Alan Prest, John Presley, and Lionel Robbins (and to the *Journal*'s referees). He is, of course, solely responsible for any errors of judgement or fact.

The author is also indebted to Professor S. R. Dennison, Robertson's literary executor, for mimeographed copies of some unpublished papers.

2.   A. Robinson, 'A Personal View', in *Essays on John Maynard Keynes*, edited by Milo Keynes (Cambridge: Cambridge University Press, 1975) p. 12.

3.   D. H. Robertson, *Essays in Monetary Theory* (London: King and Son; New York and London: Staples Press, 1940) p. 326.

4.   J. R. Hicks, 'The Monetary Theory of D. H. Robertson', *Economica*, February 1942, Vol. 9, pp. 53–7.

5.   F. Modigliani, 'The Monetarist Controversy or, Should We Foresake Stabilisation Policies?', *American Economic Review*, March 1977, 67(2), p. 1.

6.   D. H. Robertson, *A Study of Industrial Fluctuation: An Enquiry into the*

Character and Cause of the so-called Cyclical Movements of Trade (London: King & Son, 1915; reprinted with a new introduction by the London School of Economic and Political Science, 1948).

7. J. R. Presley, *Robertsonian Economics: An Examination of the Work of Sir D. H. Robertson on Industrial Fluctuation* (Macmillan; New York: Holmes and Meier, 1979).

8. A. C. Pigou, *Industrial Fluctuations* (London: Macmillan, 1927).

9. R. G. Hawtrey, *Good and Bad Trade* (London: Constable, 1913).

10. D. H. Robertson, *Banking Policy and the Price Level: An Essay in the Theory of the Trade Cycle* (London: King and Son, 1926; reprinted with a new introduction, New York: A. M. Kelley, 1949) p. 2.

11. J. Schumpeter, *Business Cycles*, 2 vols (New York: McGraw Hill, 1939).

12. M. J. Danes, 'Dennis Robertson and the Construction of Aggregative Theory', mimeographed, London School of Economics, 1979.

13. R. E. Lucas Jr. and L. A. Rapping, 'Real Wages, Employment and Inflation', *Journal of Political Economy*, September 1969, 77(5), pp. 721–54.

14. T. Mayer, *The Structure of Monetarism* (New York: Norton, 1978).

15. D. D. Purvis, 'Monetarism: A Review', *Canadian Journal of Economics*, February 1980, 13(1), pp. 6–122.

16. D. H. Robertson, 'Mr. Lloyd's Fireworks', Lecture given to the Marshall Society, Cambridge, October 1961, unpublished.

17. T. Mayer *op. cit.*, p.2.

18. R. E. Lucas Jr. and L. A. Rapping, *op. cit.* p. 748.

19. D. H. Robertson, *op. cit.*, (1940), p. 105.

20. M. Friedman and A. J. Schwartz, *A Monetary History of the United States, 1867–1960* (Princeton: Princeton University Press for the National Bureau of Economic Research, 1963); see also 'Money and Business Cycles', *Review of Economics and Statistics*, February 1963, 45(1), pt. 2, pp. 32–64.

21. M. Friedman, 'The Role of Monetary Policy', *American Economic Review*, March 1968, 58(1), pp. 7–8.

22. K. Wicksell, *Lectures in Political Economy*, Vol II, *Money*. Translated from the Swedish by E. Claassen and edited with an introduction by L. Robbins (London: Routledge & Kegan Paul; New York: Macmillan, 1955) p. 205.

23. D. Laidler, 'Mayer on Monetarism: Comments from a British Point of View', in *The Structure of Monetarism*, by T. Mayer et al. (New York: Norton, 1978) p. 135.

24. K. Brunner and A. H. Meltzer, 'Monetarism: The Principal Issues, Areas of Agreement and the Work Remaining: Reply', in *Monetarism*, J. Stein (ed.) (Amsterdam: North Holland, 1976) pp. 150–82.

25. D. H. Robertson, *Lectures on Economic Principles*. 3 vols (London: Staples Press, 1957–9; reprinted, London: Collins, Fontana Library, 1963) p. 334.

26. Ibid., p. 333.
27. Ibid., p. 345.
28. M. Friedman (ed.), *Studies in the Quantity Theory of Money* (Chicago: University of Chicago Press, 1956) p. 19.
29. R. T. Selden, 'Monetary Velocity in the United States', in M. Friedman, *op. cit.* and M. Friedman and A. Schwartz, *op. cit.*
30. D H Robertson, *Money* (New York: Harcourt Brace, 1922).
31. J. M. Keynes, *The Collected Writings of John Maynard Keynes*, Vol. 13, edited by D. Moggridge (London: Macmillan; New York: St Martin's Press; for the Royal Economic Society, 1973) p. 39.
32. Ibid., p. 40.
33. A. C. Pigou, 'The Classical Stationary State', *Economic Journal*, December 1943, 53, pp. 343–51.
34. D. H. Robertson, (1926), *op. cit.*, p. 50n.
35. D. H. Robertson, (1963), *op. cit.*, p. 421.
36. D. H. Robertson, (1940), *op. cit.*
37. M. Kalecki, *Essays in the Theory of Economic Fluctuations* (London: Allen and Unwin, 1939).
38. N. Kaldor, 'Alternative Theories of Distribution', Review of *Economic Studies*, 1955–6, 23(2), pp. 83–100.
39. T. Wilson, 'Professor Robertson on Effective Demand and the Trade Cycle', *Economic Journal*, September 1953, 63, pp. 553–78, (reprinted here pp. 97–126).
40. J. M. Keynes, *The Collected Writings of John Maynard Keynes*, Vol. 14, edited by D. Moggridge (London: Macmillan; New York: St Martin's Press; for the Royal Economic Society, 1973) p. 551.
41. D. H. Robertson, (1922), 1948, *op. cit.* p. 209.
42. D. H. Robertson, (1940), *op. cit.*, pp. 162–5.
43. J. R. Presley, *op. cit.*, p. 199.
44. J. R. Hicks, 'Mr Keynes and the "Classics": A Suggested Interpretation', *Econometrica*, April 1937, 5(2), pp. 147–59.
45. D. H. Robertson, (1940), *op. cit.*, Ch. 1 and DHR (1963), *op. cit.*, p. 376.
46. D. H. Robertson, (1963), *op. cit.*, p. 388.
47. Ibid., p. 383.
48. F. H. Hahn, 'Monetarism and Economic Theory', *Economica*, February 1980, 47(185), pp. 1–17.
49. Ibid., p. 16.
50. cf B. Kantor, 'Rational Expectations and Economic Thought', *Journal of Economic Literature*, December 1979, 17(4), pp. 1422–41.
51. T. M. Humphrey, 'Dennis H. Robertson and the Monetary Approach to Exchange Rates'. *The Federal Reserve Bank of Richmond*, Virginia, 1980 (reprinted here pp. 62–79).
52. D. H. Robertson, 'Reflections of an Ex-Magus', Lecture given to the Marshall and other societies, 1959, unpublished.

53. J. M. Keynes, *The Collected Writings of John Maynard Keynes*, Vol 29, edited by D. Moggridge (London: Macmillan: New York: St Martin's Press; for the Royal Economic Society, 1979).

54. A. C. Pigou, *Theory of Unemployment* (London: Macmillan, 1933).

55. J. M. Keynes, *The General Theory of Employment, Interest and Money* (London: Macmillan, 1936) Ch. 19.

56. D. K. Benjamin and L. A. Kochin, 'Searching for an Explanation of Unemployment in Interwar Britain', *Journal of Political Economy*, June 1979, 87(3), pp. 441–78.

57. M. Kalecki, *op. cit.*

58. J. M. Keynes, (1936), op. cit., p. 14; J. Tobin, 'Inflation and Unemployment', *American Economic Review*, March 1972, 52(1), pp. 1–18; J. A. Trevithick, 'Inflation, the Natural Unemployment Rate and the Theory of Economic Policy', *Scottish Journal of Political Economy*, February 1976, 23(1), pp. 37–57.

59. J. M. Keynes, *A Treatise on Money* (London: Macmillan, 1930).

60. UK Committee on Finance and Industry (Macmillan Committee), *Minutes of Evidence* (London: HMSO, May 8–9, 1930).

61. W. J. Fellner, 'The Robertsonian Evolution', *American Economic Review*, June 1952, 42(3), pp. 265–82.

62. D. H. Robertson, (1963), *op. cit.*, Ch. 8.

63. J. R. Presley, *op. cit.*, p. 250.

64. P. Cagan, 'Monetarism in Historical Perspective', in *The Structure of Monetarism*, by T. Mayer et al. (New York: Norton, 1978) pp. 85–93.

65. R. G. Hawtrey, *Capital and Employment* (London: Longmans, 1937) pp. 252–3.

66. J. R. Hicks, *The Crisis in Keynesian Economics* (New York: Basic Books, 1975).

67. D. H. Robertson, (1963), *op. cit.*, Ch. 7.

68. J. T. Dunlop, 'The Movement of Real and Money Wage Rates', *Economic Journal*, September 1938, 48, pp. 413–34.

69. M. Kalecki, *op. cit.*

70. J. M. Keynes, 'Relative Movements of Real Wages and Output', *Economic Journal*, March 1939, 49, pp. 34–51.

71. J. A. Trevithick, 'Money Wage Inflexibility and the Keynesian Labour Supply Function', *Economic Journal*, June 1976, 86 (342), pp. 327–32.

72. D. H. Robertson, (1940), *op. cit.*, p. 84.

73. J. R. Hicks, 'The "Classics" Again', in *Critical Essays in Monetary Theory* (Oxford: Oxford University Press, 1967) pp. 143–54.

74. A. J. Brown, *The Great Inflation 1939–1951* (London: Oxford University Press, 1955).

75. G. D. N. Worswick, 'The Great Inflation Revisited', in *Inflation, Development and Integration*. J. K. Bowers (ed.) (Leeds: Leeds University Press, 1979).

76. D H Robertson, (1959), *op. cit.*
77. UK Council On Prices, Productivity and Incomes, 1st Report (London: HMSO, 1958).
78. W. J. Fellner, 'Criteria for Demand Management Policy in View of Past Failure', in *Contemporary Economic Problems*. Edited by W. J. Fellner (Washington DC: American Enterprise Institute for Public Policy Research, 1976) pp. 85–108.
79. T. Wilson, 'Crowding Out: The Real Issues', *Banca Naz Lavoro Quarterly Review*, September 1979, (130), pp. 227–41.
80. D. H. Robertson, (1961), *op. cit.*
81. D. H. Robertson, (1963), *op. cit.*, p. 450.
82. D. H. Robertson, (1959), *op. cit.*
83. J. M. Keynes, 'On How to Avoid a Slump', reprinted from *The Times*, 12 January 1937, in *Keynes v. the 'Keynesians' . . . ? An Essay in the Thinking of J. M. Keynes and the Accuracy of the Interpretation by his followers*. By T. W. Hutchison. IEA Hobart Paperback, 11 (London: Institute of Economic Affairs, 1977) p. 66.
84. J. M. Keynes, (1973), *op. cit.*, p. 89.
85. D. H. Robertson, (1964), *op. cit.*, Ch. 8.
86. J. M. Keynes, (1977), *op. cit.*, p. 68.
87. D. H. Robertson, (1959), *op. cit.*
88. D. H. Robertson, 'The Radcliffe Report'. Lecture to the Erasmus Society, 1959.

4 Dennis H. Robertson And The Monetary Approach To Exchange Rates

Thomas M. Humphrey

Prominent among competing explanations of exchange rate determination in a regime of floating exchange rates is the so-called *monetary approach*, which holds that the exchange rate between two national currencies is determined by current and prospective relative supplies of and demands for those national money stocks. This theory has a long tradition going back more than 300 years. As an integral part of pre-Keynesian international monetary theory, it formed the central analytical core of classical and neoclassical explanations of exchange rate behaviour. Although it was temporarily eclipsed by the rival elasticities and foreign trade multiplier or income-expenditure approaches that gained popularity with the domination of the Keynesian revolution, it has recently made a comeback and today is widely employed by academic and business economists to explain the behaviour of exchange rates in the post-Bretton Woods era of generalized floating. For example, such well-known economists as Robert Barro, John Bilson, Jacob Frenkel, and Michael Mussa[1] have successfully employed the monetary approach to account for recent exchange rate experience, as have analysts at Citibank, Chase Manhattan, and other financial instituttions. Finally, it is worth noting that certain segments of the financial press, notably the editorial pages of the *Wall Street Journal*, regularly espouse the monetary approach.

Corresponding to the growing popularity of the monetary approach has been an accompanying interest in its historical antecedents. Accordingly, in the past few years Jacob Frenkel, Johan Myhrman, and Mordechai Kreinin and Lawrence Officer, respectively, have published papers dealing with the doctrinal development of that approach.[2] These papers, however, suffer from one serious omission. For while they cite several prominent economists writing in the 1920s, notably Cassel, Gregory,

Hawtrey, and Keynes, as important early proponents of the monetary approach, they say nothing about the great British economist Dennis Robertson. The result is to foster the erroneous impression that Robertson, generally recognized as one of the leading monetary theorists of the twentieth century, had virtually nothing to say about the monetary approach when in fact he was one of its principal proponents. Not only did he endorse and utilize the established components of the monetary approach, he also presaged recent developments in the theory of exchange rate expectations. For these reasons his work merits consideration.

The purpose of this chapter is twofold. First, it identifies and explains the essentials of the monetary approach to exchange rates. Second, it documents Robertson's views on that approach. This is a fairly easy task, since the bulk of Robertson's work on floating exchange rates is contained in one volume, namely the 1929 edition of his famous Cambridge Economic Handbook *Money*.[3] In that book he divides his discussion of exchange rate determination into two sections, one dealing with conditions of monetary stability and the other dealing with episodes of violent and rapid inflation. His views on the monetary approach are to be found in these two sections. What particular elements identifying the monetary approach should one look for in his view?

BASIC INGREDIENTS OF THE MONETARY APPROACH

To demonstrate that Robertson was a proponent of the monetary approach, it is necessary to spell out the key ingredients or propositions that characterize that approach.[4] These elements include the following:

Monetary View of Long Run Exchange Rate Determination

The monetary approach holds that the long run equilibrium exchange rate between two national currencies is determined chiefly by relative national money supplies and demands operating through relative national price levels. This proposition implies a particular monetary transmission mechanism or channel of causation linking money to exchange rates. Accordingly, the monetary approach specifies such a mechanism and identities quantity theory of money and purchasing power parity relationships as the key links in that mechanism. The quantity theory says that the general price level is determined by the demand adjusted money stock, i.e, by the nominal quantity of money per unit of real money demand. In other words, the price level equates money supply and demand by deflating the real value of the nominal money stock to the level people desire to hold. By contrast, the purchasing power parity doctrine states that the long-run equilibrium exchange rate tends to equal the ratio of the price levels in the two countries concerned. This condition ensures that the real (exchange rate adjusted) price of goods is everywhere the same so that there exists no arbitrage advantage to buying in one country over the other. It also ensures that both moneys have the same real (exchange rate adjusted) purchasing power such that there exists no incentive to switch from one currency to the other. Taken together, the quantity theory and purchasing power parity components imply that relative money supplies and demands operating through relative national price levels determine the long-run equilibrium exchange rates. And according to the monetary approach, the stability of that equilibrium is ensured by the self correcting characteristic of the purchasing power parity mechanism itself. Thus, should random deviations from purchasing power parity occur, they would be quickly eliminated. For by overvaluing one currency and undervaluing the other on the foreign exchanges, such deviations would shift demand from the former currency to the latter and in so doing bid the exchange rate back to purchasing power parity equilibrium.

Asset Market View of Short Run Exchange Rate Behaviour

The foregoing proposition refers to exchange rate determination in the long run when purchasing power parity holds. With respect to exchange rate determination in the short run when purchasing power parity may not hold, the monetary approach advances the so-called *asset market* view. According to that view the exchange rate between two national currencies behaves like an asset price in an efficient market, adjusting instantly to a level at which both asset (i. e., money) stocks are willingly held. As an efficient asset price, the current spot exchange rate is particularly sensitive to expectations of future exchange rates, expectations that are heavily conditioned by recent and current monetary policy and other indicators of the future course of monetary policy. More generally, as an efficient asset price, the current exchange rate embodies all available information about current and prospective events likely to affect the future external values of the two currencies and adjusts instantaneously to incorporate new information about changed conditions. In this manner new information about future exchange rates is discounted into the current exchange rate analogously to the way that news about the future profitability of a corporation is discounted into the current market price of its equity shares.

Role of Expectations

As noted above, one implication of the asset market view is that the current spot exchange rate is strongly influenced by current expectations of future exchange rates. This is so because the expected rate of change of the exchange rate is the same as the anticipated rate of return from holding foreign rather than domestic money. As such, expectations affect the relative demand for the two currencies and thereby influence the exchange rate. Thus a rise in the expected rate of depreciation of the exchange rate will, by raising the expected yield from holding foreign rather than domestic currency, shift demand from the latter to the former thereby depreciating the current spot exchange rate. In short, the spot exchange rate is determined by exchange rate expectations operating through relative money demands.

Rational Expectations Hypothesis

Besides explaining how expectations affect exchange rates, the monetary approach also explains how expectations themselves are determined. According to the monetary approach, people formulate exchange rate expectations consistent with the way that exchange rates are actually determined in the economy. Thus, if actual observed exchange rates are determined by money supply and demand, it follows that expected future exchange rates are determined by forecasts of future values of those same monetary variables. In particular, the monetary approach maintains that exchange rate expectations are governed by expectations of future money supplies per unit of real money demands. These latter expectations, the monetary approach asserts, are formed from all available information about prospective events likely to influence future money supplies and demands. In so arguing, the monetary approach advances the *rational expectations hypothesis* according to which the market's predictions of future exchange rates are the same as those generated by the actual mechanism that determines exchange rates. This assumption ensures that the monetary approach is internally consistent, i.e., that its explanation of expectations formation is consistent with its explanation of exchange rate determination. Such consistency is thought to be characteristic of the forecasting behaviour of rational agents who use knowledge of the actual exchange rate generating mechanism in formulating expectations of future exchange rates. Knowing that money supplies and demands determine actual exchange rates, rational agents will predict future exchange rates from forecasts of future money supplies and demands.

Constituting the central analytical core of the modern monetary approach to floating exchange rates, the foregoing ingredients must be found in Robertson's work if he is to be judged a proponent of that approach. Accordingly, the following paragraphs show what he had to say on each of the propositions listed above.

Before discussing Robertson's views, however, it should be pointed out that the long-run quantity theory version of the monetary approach (i. e., the first proposition above) long predates him. That version dates back at least to the mid-sixteenth century, when Spanish scholastic writers of the Salamanca School used it to explain fluctuations in the Spanish currency price of Flemish money.[5] And in the famous Bank Restriction Controversy of the early 1800s, David Ricardo, John Wheatley, and other bullionist writers employed it to explain the fall of the paper pound on the foreign exchanges following Britain's switch from fixed to floating exchange rates during the Napoleonic wars.[6] The theory was endorsed by A. Marshall in the late 1880s and revived by Gustav Cassel in 1916 to explain exchange rate movements during World War One.[7] After the war the theory was widely used to explain the fall of the German mark in the famous hyperinflation episode of the early 1920s.[8] Robertson, of course, was well aware of this and goes out of his way to disclaim any originality in his presentation of the theory. His views on this long-established or 'customary' (as he called it) doctrine are presented immediately below.[9]

LONG-RUN EQUILIBRIUM EXCHANGE RATE

The first proposition of the monetary approach states that the long-run equilibrium exchange rate between two national currencies is determined by the relative supplies of and demands for those national money stocks. That Robertson was in basic agreement with this proposition is evident from his discussion of the determination of the 'normal level of the rate of exchange' between two inconvertible paper currencies (or 'arbitrary independent standards' as he called them).[10] In his discussion he attributes the state of the exchanges largely to the underlying monetary conditions in the two countries concerned. Although he denies that these monetary factors are the sole determinants of exchange rates, he repeatedly refers to them as the dominant determinants. For example, in various places he specifically identifies 'the monetary situation' or 'the supply of money in the two countries' or 'the state of a country's monetary glands' as 'the essential condition for the maintenance of a given rate of exchange'.[11] Elsewhere, when discussing the stability of exchange rate equilibrium, he reiterates his belief in the importance of the monetary factor when he notes that the exchange rate must always gravitate to that particular equilibrium level 'which the existing money supply of the country as compared with that of other countries renders permanently maintainable'.[12]

Embodied in the monetary approach is a particular model of the monetary transmission mechanism connecting money with exchange rates. As usually presented, that model contains quantity theory of money and purchasing power parity relationships, the former linking money supplies and demands to prices and the latter linking prices to the exchange rate. These same elements can be found in Robertson's work. Consistent with the monetary approach, he combines them to arrive at the conclusion that exchange rates are determined largely by relative money supplies and demands operating through price levels particularly the prices of internationally traded goods. He reaches this conclusion via the following route.

First, he argues that 'the value of money . . . depends on the conditions of demand for it and the quantity of it available'.[13] This of course is the quantity theory of money which may be written as

$$(1) \quad P = M/D$$

where P is the general price level (the inverse of the value of money), M the nominal money stock, and D the real demand for money. This equation, which says that the price level is determined by and varies equiproportionally with the stock of money per unit of real money demand, is expressed by Robertson in the following words: 'given the conditions of demand for money . . . the general level of prices varies directly as the quantity of money available'.[14] Note that equation (1), which may be written as $M/P = D$, also says that the price level adjusts to equate the real (price deflated) value of the nominal money stock with the public's real demand for it, thereby clearing the market for real cash balances. Consistent with his adherence to the quantity theory. Robertson employs this alternative interpretation when he declares that, given the public's real demand for money, a 10 per cent rise in the nominal money stock will produce a corresponding 10 per cent rise in the price level such that the price deflated or 'aggregate real value of the public's money supply is no greater than it was before'.[15]

Second, he presents the purchasing power parity relationship, stating that 'the normal level of the rate of exchange depends on the relative price levels, in the money of the two countries, of the things which enter into trade between them'.[16] This of course is the traded goods or commodity arbitrage version of purchasing power parity, which holds the equilibrium exchange rate is equal to the ratio of the domestic and foreign price levels of internationally traded goods. In symbols

$$(2) \quad E = P_T / P_T^*$$

where E is the exchange rate (defined as the domestic currency price of a unit of foreign currency), and PT and P_T^* are the domestic and foreign currency prices of traded goods, respectively.

Third, he assumes that in long-run equilibrium the price of traded goods bears a certain equilibrium relationship to the general price level. This relationship can be expressed as

$$(3) \ P_T = RP$$

where R denotes the equilibrium ratio of traded-goods prices to general prices in the home country, as can be seen by rewriting the equation in the form $R = P_T/P$. Representing the relative price of traded goods in terms of the general price level, this equation summarizes the equilibrium *structure* of prices in the home country. This notion of a stable equilibrium price structure can be inferred from Robertson's statement that he is assuming conditions of 'comparative stability' characterized by the absence of 'violent and continuous monetary dislocation'.[17] It can also be inferred from his willingness to substitute traded goods prices interchangeably for general prices as a measure of the value of money.[18]

Fourth, he substitutes equations (1) and (3) into equation (2) to obtain the following result

$$(4) \ E = (1/P_T^*)R\frac{M}{D}$$

which says that given foreign prices and the domestic price structure the exchange rate depends on the domestic money supply per unit of real money demand. Robertson states this result when he declares that 'given the price level of traded goods in terms of utopes [Robertson's hypothetical foreign currency] . . . the monetary situation in England turns out to be the essential condition for the maintenance of a given rate of exchange'.[19]

Finally, he assumes that prices in the foreign country are determined analogously to their domestic counterparts. Specifically, the foreign price of traded goods is linked through a price structure variable to the foreign general price level which is determined by foreign money supply and demand. Substituting this assumption into equation (4) yields the following expression

$$(5) \ E = \frac{R}{R*} \ \frac{D*}{D} \ \frac{M}{M*}$$

which says that the long-run equilibrium exchange rate is determined by the product of three groups of factors, namely relative price structures, relative real money demands, and relative nominal money supplies, respectively.[20] Of these three groups, the first two capture the effect of real (nonmonetary) influences on the exchange rate while the third captures purely monetary influences.

Equation (5), which summarizes Robertson's theory of long-run exchange rate determination, puts him squarely in the ranks of the monetary approach. To be sure, the equation does contain a relative price structure variable (and hence an extra channel through which real factors can affect exchange rates) not usually found in the monetary approach. Apart from this, however, the equation is exactly the same as that advanced by the monetary approach. It embodies the latter's assumption of quantity theory and purchasing power parity linkages running from money to the exchange rate, and therefore, in Robertson's words, 'serves to remind us that the exchange rates are . . . connected with the supply of money in the two countries'.[21] Moreover, like the monetary approach, it identifies relative money demands and supplies as key determinants of the exchange rate. Finally, it yields the standard monetarist homogeneity postulate that a *ceteris paribus* rise in the relative money supply produces an equi-proportional rise in the nominal exchange rate. That Robertson accepts this homogeneity postulate is evident from his statement that if 'the supply of Utopian money had become double . . . while neither the supply of English money nor any other conditions of the problem had changed, we should not be surprised to learn that the rate of exchange had become 10 utopes to the pound instead of 5'.[22] In short, to the extent he accepts these features, Robertson is a proponent of the monetary approach.

Before concluding this section, it is necessary to compare Robertson's views of the purchasing power parity relationship with those of the monetary approach. Regarding purchasing power parity there are at least three main issues, the first referring to the relevant price levels to use in calculating the parity. On this issue Robertson disagrees with the monetary approach. For whereas the latter holds that general prices should be employed in computing the purchasing power parity, Robertson argues that only the prices of internationally-traded goods should be used. Thus in stating that the equilibrium exchange rate tends to equal the ratio of domestic to foreign prices, he makes it emphatically clear that he is referring to the prices of 'traded goods' or 'those goods which are the subject of trade'.[23] He apparently believes that purchasing power parity logically holds only for prices subject to internaional equalization by commodity arbitrage, for he states that it is only the movement of such prices 'which we should expect to correspond closely to the movements of the exchanges'.[24] Not mentioned by him is a point stressed by the monetary approach, namely that, with intercommodity substitution in production and consumption and interindustry competition for factors of production, the prices of traded and nontraded goods tend to be sufficiently closely related such that general prices can be used to approximate the purchasing power parity. Nevertheless, on at least one occasion he apparently accepts this proposition. For he uses a general price index to proxy the purchasing power parity claiming that, as a practical matter, the index is 'good enough . . . to illustrate the general normal relation between price levels and exchanges'.[25]

The second issue relating to purchasing power parity concerns the purpose or role of the exchange rate. On this issue the monetary approach contends that the chief function of the exchange rate is to clear the market for money balances by equating the real purchasing power of both currencies such that both money stocks are willingly held. That Robertson is in substantial agreement with this point can be inferred from such comments of his as 'the normal rate of exchange between [two countries] depends on the relative values of their moneys in terms of traded goods', and 'the normal rate . . . reflects the condition of the country's money supply as compared with that of the other countries'.[26] The first comment implies that the purchasing power parity exchange rate embodies the relative price deflator that, when applied to relative nominal national money supplies, serves to equalize the real (price deflated) value of money across nations. Robertson's second comment implies that exchange rates, like prices, also summarize the underlying monetary conditions in each country. Both implications are consistent with the notion that the exchange rate functions to clear the market for national money balances by equating the real purchasing power of both currencies such that there exists no incentive to switch from one currency to the other.

Robertson recognizes, as do proponents of the monetary approach, that the exchange rate also plays a commodity arbitrage role, adjusting to equalize the real price of traded goods across nations so that there exists no advantage to buying in one market over another. In this connection he points out that if the real price of goods were to differ between countries such that it became advantageous to buy in the cheaper country and sell in the dear one, the resulting excess demand for the currency of the former country would quickly bid the exchange rate up to the purchasing power parity level at which the common currency prices of goods are everywhere the same. While recognizing the arbitrage function of the exchange rate, however, he nevertheless apparently places greater emphasis on its money market clearing role. For whereas he mentions the commodity arbitrage role but once, he repeatedly contends that the equilibrium exchange rate must be consistent with the underlying monetary conditions in the countries concerned.[27] In so doing, he implicitly endorses the proposition that the chief function of the exchange rate is to achieve international monetary equilibrium by clearing the markets for national money balances.

As for the third issue, namely whether the purchasing power parity is an equilibrium condition or a cause-and-effect relationship between prices and exchange rate, Robertson obviously holds it to be the former. In so doing, he agrees with the monetary approach. Like proponents of that approach, he maintains that prices and the exchange rate are both endogenous variables simultaneously determined by underlying monetary conditions. As he puts it, both variables are 'rendered possible by the monetary situation', i.e., both are established at levels 'which the existing money supply of the country, as compared with that of other countries, renders permanently maintainable'.[28] In short, on this issue as with most of the others, Robertson adheres to the monetary approach.

ASSET MARKET VIEW

The second component of the monetary approach is the asset market view, according to which the exchange rate behaves like an efficient asset price, embodying all available information about the future values of the currencies and adjusting instantaneously to incorporate new information about changed circumstances. Robertson possessed a sophisticated understanding of the asset market view, which he used in explaining 'the misbehaviour of the foreign exchanges' during the post World War One hyperinflation episodes of the early 1920s. For example, regarding the proposition that the current exchange rate registers the market's perceptions about the future exchange rate, i.e., that market participants discount the expected future value of the currencies into the current spot exchange rate – he says that exchange rates tend 'to reflect the degrees of confidence felt in the future of a country's money by the nimble-witted dealers in exchange'.[29] These dealers he describes as being especially 'well informed and impressionable' implying that, consistent with the concept of an efficient market, they utilize all available information in predicting future exchange rates.[30]

As for the speed of adjustment of exchange rates in response to new information, Robertson implies that adjustment is virtually instantaneous. For 'if a country is rapidly increasing its supply of money', he says, a 'lack of confidence in the future of the money . . . strikes like a flash upon the consciousness of the well informed and impressionable gentlemen whose business it is to carry on dealings in foreign money'.[31] As a result, these dealers 'become highly willing to buy foreign money and to sell the money of their own country' and in so doing immediately bid up the exchange rate.[32] In this manner new information about the likely future value of the currencies is immediately impounded in the current spot exchange rate, which adjusts instantly to its new equilibrium level consistent with anticipated future monetary conditions.

Having developed the asset market view, Robertson used it to explain why the *external* value of a currency (i.e., its value on the foreign exchanges) could temporarily depreciate faster than its internal value (i.e., its value in domestic commodity markets) during periods of rapid inflation. In so doing he presents the rudiments of a theory of differential speeds of price adjustment in asset and commodity markets, respectively. According to him, whereas the exchange rate adjusts instantaneously to changes in expectations of future monetary conditions, the prices of 'home produced goods and services' adjust slowly, i.e., they 'come lumbering after' the exchange rate with a lag.[33] In other words, the market for foreign exchange is more efficient than domestic commodity markets in exploiting new information about future prospects. For this reason, expectations are discounted into exchange rates prior to being discounted into domestic commodity prices and 'the external value of a country's money falls faster than the internal'.[34]

Robertson's views on asset and commodity price adjustment sound remarkably like those of the monetary approach. The same conclusions, namely that differential speeds of price response cause the exchange rate to adjust faster than commodity prices and thereby produce temporary disparities between the external and internal values of the currency, continue to be voiced by modern proponents of the monetary approach. Here, for example, is what one of those proponents, M. Mussa, has to say on the subject:

> Relative adjustment speeds of price . . . in different markets are of vital importance in understanding fluctuations in exchange rates . . . In the asset market approach to exchange rate theory, it is asserted that the exchange rate is a relative asset price that is determined primarily by conditions of equilibrium in the market for asset stocks. What this means is that the exchange rate . . . responds essentially instantaneously to changes in economic conditions, in particular, to new information that is received by market participants. Of course, exchange rates are also related to general price levels. . . . But, if price levels adjust relatively slowly in comparison with exchange rates, then . . . exchange rate movements should frequently anticipate, rather than follow, movements in national price levels.[35]

In short, because the exchange rate responds more rapidly to news about future events than do commodity prices, the external value of the currency deviates temporarily from its internal value. On this point Robertson and Mussa agree.

Prior to ending this section, it should be pointed out that Robertson was not alone in endorsing the asset market view of exchange rates in the 1920s. Gustav Cassel, for example, also enunciated it. Perhaps its strongest proponent, however, was Ludwig von Mises, whose contributions to the monetary approach, like those of Robertson, have been largely overlooked. As early as 1919 von Mises wrote that exchange rates, like the prices of other assets traded on organized markets, 'are speculative rates of exchange', that they reflect 'not only the present but also potential future development', and that they respond to news of excessive monetary growth 'relatively soon . . . long before the prices of other goods and services'.[36] Again, in 1923, he wrote that the current spot exchange rate 'forecasts anticipated future changes in commodity prices'; that it is 'determined by nothing more than the anticipated future purchasing power attributed to a unit of each currency', and that it adjusts faster than commodity prices to news about future events.[37] Any notion that the asset market view is a recent development is quickly dispelled by a reading of Robertson and von Mises.

ROLE OF EXPECTATIONS

The third proposition of the monetary approach deals with exchange rate expectations. Consistent with the monetary approach, Robertson recognized that expectations play a central role in shortrun exchange rate determination. In so doing he implicitly accepted the proposition that the expected future rate of change of the exchange rate constitutes the expected cost of holding one currency rather than the other, and therefore affects the current spot exchange rate through relative money demands. To be sure, he did not state this proposition explicitly. That is, he did not specify the expected rate of change of the exchange rate as a cost or rate of return variable in the money demand function. He did, however, assume that the demand for money in each country is affected by the expected rate of inflation in that country.[38] By implication, however, this means that relative money demands are affected by expected inflation differentials. And since the expected inflation differential is closely related to the expected future rate of depreciation of the exchange rate, he implicitly reached the conclusion that expectations of exchange rate depreciation affect the current exchange rate through the channel of relative money demands. In particular, he argued that if everybody expects the currency to depreciate, they will attempt to get out of that currency into other assets, including foreign exchange. The resulting reduction in the demand for the currency will produce the very depreciation that is anticipated. In his own words, if the public expects a depreciation of the currency, 'every individual passes it on as quickly as he is able, knowing that if he keeps it it will lose value still further in his hands, and seeks with ingenuity and persistence to embody his resources in any other form'.[39] One of these forms is foreign exchange. Consequently, people 'become largely willing to buy foreign money and to sell the money of their own country' and 'this involves their coming on to the exchange market as purchasers of foreign money'.[40] The resulting reduction in the demand for domestic relative to foreign money causes the exchange rate to depreciate. On this point Robertson is in perfect agreement with the monetary approach.

RATIONAL EXPECTATIONS HYPOTHESIS

Finally, Robertson endorsed the last ingredient of the monetary approach, namely the rational expectations hypothesis. The latter states that people formulate exchange rate expectations from information about prospective policy actions and other events believed to have a bearing on the future values of the monetary variables that actually determine exchange rates. Knowing that monetary policies are a basic determinant of long-run equilibrium exchange rates, rational agents will predict future equilibrium exchange rates from forecasts of future monetary policies and these forecasts will be immediately discounted into the current spot exchange rate. That this was indeed Robertson's view is evident from his statement that 'the actual rate of exchange is largely governed by the *expected* behaviour of the country's monetary authority'.[41] The same idea was expressed by von Mises, who declared that the exchange rate 'is affected only by changes in the relation between the demand for, and quantity of, money and the prevailing opinion with respect to expected changes in that relationship, including those produced by governmental monetary policies'.[42]

Robertson also stressed that exchange rate changes largely stem from *unexpected* policy actions. In his words, if the monetary 'authority behaves in a way which is not expected, the rate will ultimately alter'.[43] In stating this point Robertson presaged the monetary approach's distinction between the effects of expected versus unexpected policies, respectively. According to this distinction, expected policy actions should have little or no impact on the exchange rate since those policies have already been fully anticipated and discounted into the exchange rate.

Having been foreseen in advance, such policies entail no disappointed expectations, no surprises, no new information to discount into the exchange rate. By contrast, unexpected policies should indeed affect the exchange rate. Not having been foreseen in advance, they produce forecasting errors that constitute new information that the market discounts into the exchange rate. In this manner they alter the exchange rate, which adjusts to incorporate the new information represented by the policy surprises. In recognizing this point Robertson foreshadowed much of the recent research on rational expectations.

CONCLUSION

The preceding has identified four basic essentials of the monetary approach to exchange rates and has documented Robertson's views on each. His writings indicate that he largely accepted these essentials and that he incorporated them into his own analysis of the foreign exchanges. Moreover, with respect to the asset market and rational expectations components, he contributed insights that are remarkably suggestive of recent work. All in all, his position is consistent with the monetary approach. This is not to say, however, that everything he wrote conformed to the monetary approach. On the contrary, at one point he used the rival elasticities approach to deny the existence of a stable equilibrium exchange rate.[44] At another point he suggested, contrary to the monetary approach, that national money stocks may be endogenous rather than exogenous variables.[45] Nor is it to claim that he was the only economist in the 1920s to recognize and discuss all the ingredients of the monetary approach. Ludwig von Mises, for one, enunciated them even more emphatically and lucidly than Robertson. Nevertheless, Robertson did endorse and utilize these ingredients and for that reason deserves to be recognized along with Cassel, Hawtrey, Keynes, and von Mises as one of the important early proponents of the monetary approach.

NOTES

1.   J. Bilson, 'Recent Developments in Monetary Models of Exchange Rate Determination', *IMF Staff Papers*, 26 (2), June 1979, pp. 201–23; J. Frenkel, 'A Monetary Approach to the Exchange Rate: Doctrinal Aspects and Empirical Evidence', *Scandinavian Journal of Economics*, 78, (2), May 1976, pp. 200–24; J. Frenkel and K. Clements, 'Exchange Rates in the 1990's: A Monetary Approach', Working Paper 290, *NBER Working Paper Series* (Cambridge: National Bureau of Economic Research, October 1978); M. Mussa, 'The Exchange Rate, the Balance of Payments and Monetary and Fiscal Policy under a Regime of Controlled Floating', *Scandinavian Journal of Economics*, 78 (2), May 1976, pp. 229–48; M. Mussa, 'Empirical Regularities in the Behavior of Exchange Rates and Theories of the Foreign Exchange Market', vol. 11 of the *Carnegie-Rochester Conference Series on Public Policy*, a supplementary series to the *Journal of Monetary Economics*, 1979, pp. 9–57; M. Mussa, 'Macroeconomic Interdependence and the Exchange Rate', in R. Dornbusch and J. Frenkel (eds) in *International Economic Policy: Theory and Evidence* (Baltimore: Johns Hopkins University Press, 1979).
2.   J. Frenkel, *op. cit.*; J. Myhrman, 'Experiences of Flexible Exchange Rates in Earlier Periods: Theories, Evidence and a New View', *Scandinavian Journal of Economics*, 78, (2), May 1976, pp. 169–96; M. Kreinin and L. Officer, *The Monetary Approach to the Balance of Payments: A Survey*, Princeton Studies in International Finance, 43 (Princeton, NJ: Princeton University, International Finance Section, 1978) see especially pp. 28–31.
3.   D. H. Robertson, *Money* (New York: Harcourt Brace & Co, 1922). Unless otherwise noted, all references are to the 1963 reprint of the 1947 edition, which is virtually the same as the 1929 edition as far as the discussion of floating exchange rates is concerned.
4.   The essentials of the modern monetary approach are expounded more fully in Bilson, *op. cit.*; Frenkel, *op. cit.*; Frenkel and Clements, *op. cit.*; and Mussa *op. cit.*
5.   M. Grice-Hutchinson, *The School of Salamanca: Readings in Spanish Monetary Theory, 1544–1605* (Oxford: Clarendon Press, 1952).
6.   J. Myhrman, *op. cit.*, pp. 170–3.
7.   Ibid., pp. 177–8; E Eshag, *From Marshall to Keynes: An Essay on The Monetary Theory of the Cambridge School* (Oxford: Basil Blackwell, 1963) pp. 26–34.
8.   H. Ellis, *German Monetary Theory, 1905–1933* (Cambridge, Mass.: Harvard University Press, 1934) pp. 209–36.
9.   D. H. Robertson, *Money*, 4th ed. (Chicago: University of Chicago Press, 1963) p. 58.
10.   Ibid., pp. 57–8.

11. Ibid., p. 60, p. 103.
12. Ibid., p. 101.
13. Ibid., p. 32.
14. Ibid., p. 26.
15. Ibid., p. 76.
16. Ibid., p. 58.
17. Ibid., p. 58.
18. See Robertson ibid., p. 61 where he refers to the value of money measured "in terms of traded goods."
19. Ibid., p. 60.
20. Asterisks refer to foreign country variables.
21. D. H. Robertson, (1963), *op. cit.*, p. 60.
22. Ibid., p. 60.
23. Ibid., pp. 60–1.
24. D. H. Robertson, (1922), *op. cit.*, p. 141.
25. Ibid., p. 141.
26. D. H. Robertson, (1963), *op. cit.*, pp. 61, 102.
27. Ibid., pp. 59–61, p. 101, p. 103.
28. Ibid., pp. 60, 101.
29. Ibid., p. 101.
30. Ibid., p. 99.
31. Ibid., p. 99.
32. Ibid., p. 99.
33. Ibid., p. 101.
34. Ibid., pp. 101, 108.
35. M. Mussa, *op. cit.*, pp. 196–7.
36. L. von Mises, 'Balance of Payments and Foreign Exchange Rates' (1919) and 'Stabilization of the Monetary Unit from the Viewpoint of Theory' (1923), both in L. von Mises, *On the Manipulation of Money and Credit* (trans. Bettina Bien Greaves, ed. Percy L. Greaves, Jr) (Dobbs Ferry, NY: Free Market Books, 1978) p. 51.
37. L. von Mises, (1923), Ibid., pp. 28–31.
38. D. H. Robertson, (1963), *op. cit.*, pp. 97–8.
39. Ibid., p. 98.
40. Ibid., p. 99.
41. Ibid., p. 102.
42. L. von Mises, *op. cit.*, p. 25.
43. D. H. Robertson, (1963), *op. cit.*, p. 102.
44. Ibid., p. 100.
45. Ibid., p. 102.

5 J. M. Keynes and D. H. Robertson: Three Phases Of Collaboration
John R. Presley

INTRODUCTION

Academic interest in the working relationship between Keynes and Robertson has, not surprisingly, focused upon their disagreements over the writing of *The General Theory* (hereafter *GT*).[1] While not disputing that the period from 1931–5 was the most productive and relevant period in the formulation of 'Keynesian Economics', such a focus does disguise the close and substantive collaboration which existed between Keynes and Robertson throughout the 1920s and to a lesser extent from 1910–15. The purpose of this paper therefore is to redress the balance, to examine the ebb and flow of ideas between them which culminated in such major books as *Banking Policy and the Price Level* (hereafter *BPPL*)[2] and *The Treatise on Money* (hereafter *TM*).[3] The *GT* was the finale in Keynes's presentation of his macroeconomic thinking, but certainly not his only major contribution; although it could be argued that the *GT* was not totally consistent with what Keynes had written before, nevertheless his earlier work, with Robertson and others, did have some bearing upon the *GT* and to that extent is important. The *GT* represented the end product of over a quarter of a century of Keynes's thoughts on macroeconomic theory, and it was upon this solid foundation that the *GT* was constructed. Clearly for Robertson, as will be seen in the final section here, the *GT* was an inadequate ending to their collaborative efforts; for Keynesian economists it symbolized the beginning of a totally new approach to macroeconomics and unfortunately this led to a relative neglect of what had gone before. Yet one is reminded of Hicks' comment on the *GT*:

the effect on Mr Kaldor's mind, as well as on my own, of the *GT* has been profound; but we have each of us been led, sometimes consciously, sometimes unconsciously, through Keynes to Robertson.[4]

Equally, as the following pages demonstrate, Hicks could have argued that he was led back to the pre-*GT* Keynes who shared much common ground with D. H. Robertson from 1910 to 1930.

The chapter is divided into three parts. The first section looks at the period of early collaboration (1910–15); the second examines the more significant period of joint work from *Money*[5] and *The Tract on Monetary Reform* (hereafter *TMR*)[6] through to *TM*; the third considers their conflict over the drafts of the *GT* and Robertson's reaction to it. The paper concentrates throughout upon their work in the area of macroeconomic theory and policy.

Robertson devoted most of his working life to the study of industrial fluctuation but wrote also on many topics of mutual interest to Keynes. Although the impression of academic disagreement will be given in the third section (pp. 90–3) here, it must be stressed at the outset that they shared common views on many topics outside of macroeconomic theory; there was little dispute over policy, over the consequences of World War One or the return to the gold standard, all controversial issues of their day. Indeed, in essence there was a fourth phase of collaboration in the post-war period when Keynes and Robertson worked together at Bretton Woods. Although this gave little opportunity for reconciliation over the *GT*, it did nevertheless show the strength of their like-mindedness on the international monetary order.[7]

TEACHER AND STUDENT 1910–15

This is the most neglected period of their working relationship and rarely merits recognition in contemporary literature, yet in terms of its significance for the evolution of their respective theories it is very important.

Keynes became Robertson's Director of Studies at Trinity College, Cambridge, in 1910 when Robertson transferred from the classics to the economics tripos. Keynes was seven years older than Robertson; he graduated from Cambridge in mathematics in 1905. By 1912 Robertson had gained a first in the economics tripos and two years later was able to submit a thesis on industrial fluctuation which earned for him a Trinity fellowship. Their relationship during this period was very much one of student and tutor. Robertson was required to submit essays to Keynes. These essays (some of which survive) are 'rather remarkable for a young man whose knowledge of economics was at first derived from reading Marshall's *Principles* and the *Wealth of Nations* during the previous summer vacation' but they are on 'standard Marshallian topics (e.g., theory of rent) and have no relevance to later work, especially industrial fluctuation'.[8]

Their major early collaborations concerned the drafts of *A Study of Industrial Fluctuation* (hereafter *Study*).[9] Robertson's thesis impressed Keynes as a 'most brilliant and important contribution to the subject'.[10] Despite this, Keynes was not prepared to support it fully as an explanation of the trade cycle, although he did remark 'your work has suggested to me what appears at first sight a superb theory about fluctuations'.[11]

This 'superb theory' was presented at the Political Economy Club's meeting on 3 December 1913 in London. In many ways this was the first step towards Keynes's *TMR*, although it specifically addressed the question of the responsibility of bankers for industrial fluctuations.[12]

Keynes's paper exhibits a number of interesting features. First, it rejects the type of over-investment theory associated with Robertson's *Study* on the grounds that it contains two invalid suggestions; that more capital can be invested than exists and that more investment is made than is profitable. Keynes proceeds to uphold the 'real saving' doctrine (see later) and counteracts the second suggestion by an appeal to the facts. Secondly, Keynes distrusts the monetary explanation of the cycle which emphasises the fluctuation in bank credit as the cause of cyclical movements. This, at that time, was associated with both Fisher and Hawtrey. Consequently Keynes had to provide an alternative explanation and this is found within the behaviour of the banks.

Resources in any period are either spent, saved or 'suspended', that is either held in the banks or hoarded. Investment is financed from two sources, from that part of existing resources saved by individuals or from part of the 'suspended' resources made available by the banks for investment. It is the second source which promotes a tendency to over-investment during the upswing of the cycle: 'If no one who directs capital operations could obtain funds except by inducing someone who had saved them to place them with him, clearly investment could never in a period exceed saving. The machinery of banking, however, permits this'. Banks allow those who invest to 'encroach on the community's reserves of free capital'.[13]

Robertson was not sufficiently persuaded by this paper to make fundamental revisions to his *Study* before publication. He was more preoccupied than Keynes with the causes of the upturn in the cycle. These were the real factors promoting the initial change in investment, not those which caused over-investment to take place and the downturn to follow. Keynes did, however, accept that the growth of more profitable investment opportunities through invention and the opening up of new territories (and changes brought about by, for example, wars) could stimulate investment. This approach is totally consistent with the *Study* and was indeed the major feature of the real over-investment theory put forward by Robertson. Robertson in 1915 chose also to stress the role of agricultural change in encouraging a burst of investment out of depression. For him there were more fundamental causes of over-investment than those isolated by Keynes: in fact, it was inherent in the capitalist system of production; the nature of capital goods, their indivisibility, their long gestation period and the consequent uncertainty which surrounded the investment process were central to the generation of too much investment and the downturn.

Although Keynes had based his approach in no small degree upon the drafts of the *Study*, Robertson, in turn, had a reciprocal obligation to Keynes, acknowledged in the published version of the *Study* and in later work. Keynes's paper exhibits some characteristics which Robertson was to develop later in *Money* and in *BPPL*; in particular, one can recognise the embryo of the forced saving thesis which Robertson was to elaborate more comprehensively in the concepts of automatic and induced 'lacking' in *BPPL*. Keynes believed that saving and investment need not be equal; during a boom investment would exceed voluntary saving, the deficiency being accounted for by the ability of the banks to transfer 'suspended' resources to investment. In the *Study* Robertson wrote 'to the latter (Mr J. M. Keynes) I owe more than it would be possible to acknowledge'.[14] Undoubtedly, Keynes had helped refine

Robertson's thesis, although there is little to support this claim either in correspondence or within the text of the *Study*. What is evident, however, is the partial acceptance in the *Study* of the 'real saving' doctrine advocated by Keynes in 1913. In this the amount of saving which can finance investment is equated with the accumulated stocks of consumer goods. This is consistent with Robertson's desire to get behind the monetary veil to the real determinants of the cycle in the *Study*. This contrasts with the approach of, for example, Tugan Baranowski, where savings were equated with loanable funds rather than with the real stock of consumer goods which allow an economy to divert a larger proportion of its resources to investment.

It would be incorrect to claim that Keynes was the only influence upon Robertson in this respect for he had, by 1913, already discovered a more lucid account of the 'real saving' doctrine in the work of Marcel Labordère[15] and also in a summary of Spiethoff's theory.[16] Nevertheless he did thank Keynes for furnishing him with the understanding that crisis could be caused by too rapid a utilization of the stock of consumer goods in the process of redistributing production more towards capital goods.[17] But clearly Robertson was less convinced by this argument than Keynes: 'he is, I think, mistaken in conveying the impression that the relapse of investment is always due to the physical impossibility of maintaining it upon the existing scale'.[18] Of more importance to Robertson, over-investment is defined not in relation to the supply of real saving but in terms of the inadequate demand for capital goods relative to their supply at the peak of the cycle. Indeed, the crisis could occur even where the stock of consumer goods was relatively high.

Keynes's exposure to the *Study* did not persuade him of the virtues of public finance at that stage and certainly there was no reference to Robertson's *Study* in this respect in his later writings on fiscal measures. D. H. Robertson had been very supportive of public spending as a cure for depression; this was a natural consequence of the over-investment theory of industrial fluctuation which he presented.

Unemployment was the direct result of a deficient demand for capital goods and the solution therefore lay in 'an artificial elevation in the demand for constructional goods'.[19] He did not claim any originality for this policy cure, accepting the similar recommendation of the Minority Report of the Poor Law Commissioners which had preceded the *Study*. Public works policies in a depression became a persistent recommendation by Robertson throughout his lifetime. He was the strongest critic of the so-called 'Treasury View'; as for Keynes, his advocacy of fiscal measures did not really appear until 1924.[20]

Of course the over-investment theory was indicative of one major characteristic of Robertson's work which Keynes was later to appreciate. The emphasis upon the lumpiness of investment, the long gestation period and the indivisibility of the production process, as well as the role of invention, innovation and agricultural change in the *Study*, led Robertson to have little respect for Say's Law and the associated, so-called 'classical' disposition to see an automatic movement to full employment in a capitalist economy.

Keynes was later to write 'I regard Mr Hawtrey as my grandparent and Mr Robertson as my parent in the paths of errancy'.[21] It was Robertson who had persuaded him to stray from the classical fold. Later, in *BPPL*, Robertson was to enlarge upon this continuous failure of a capitalist economy to achieve the objective of full employment.

He chose to distinguish between appropriate and inappropriate fluctuations; it was the objective of society to get rid of inappropriate fluctuation caused by errors of optimism and pessimism on the part of businessmen, or by monetary overexpansion or contraction. But to try to avoid 'appropriate' fluctuations was tantamount to preventing economic progress; industrial fluctuation was inevitable: 'out of the welter of industrial dislocation the great permanent riches of the future are generated'.[22] It is this view of the capitalist economy expressed by Robertson in 1915 and remaining with him throughout his life, which goes some way to explaining his lack of acceptance of the approach within the *GT*. Robertson believed a static economic equilibrium was never attainable; economic life was continuously changing and the analysis undertaken by economists must reflect this.

One can also observe no great preoccupation with the price level in the *Study*; Robertson was primarily concerned with industrial fluctuation, with cycles in real output. Economists are accustomed to applauding Keynes for shaking off the shackles of the classical obsession with the price level; he was to do this in 1936, Robertson had done it in 1915, surprisingly under the influence of A. C. Pigou.[23]

Keynes's 1913 paper on industrial fluctuation, brief as it was, could not have incorporated all of Robertson's main points in the voluminous drafts of the *Study*. Keynes's paper was not a policy paper, and indeed

Keynes did not write a substantial piece on economic policy until *TMR*.[24] *TMR* however took the stance of his 1913 paper, blaming industrial fluctuation on the poor bankers and consequently recommending monetary, not fiscal policy; there is little evidence to suggest that it had been influenced significantly by the *Study*.

INTO THE 1920s: CARRYING THE FLAG FORWARD

In 1947 Robertson looked back on the prewar period and declared:

> In the early 1910s and again in the 1920s I did do a bit of scrambling towards the frontier (of economic thought), firmly roped to the man of genius (Keynes) who has perished there. Sometimes, I venture to think, I was even a little bit in front of him; but in the end he went on beyond me and it is my belief – an unpopular one, I know, but I cannot help it – that he got a bit off the track and set the flag in places where it is not destined to rest.[25]

Although many would dispute the strength of Robertson's contribution to the study of industrial fluctuation, few would deny that the *Study* and *BPPL* did represent significant departures from what had gone before, particularly in the British literature.

The 1920s are remarkable for the spirit of cooperation which existed between Robertson and Keynes and the sharp contrast with their relationship in the 1930s. Their two minds worked in similar directions throughout the period until the final version of *TM* was published and the first major sign of academic disagreement appeared. Reading Keynes's *Collected Writings*, vol. XIII, it is difficult to disentangle the sources of the many original ideas which they put forward in the 1920s. They acted as a stimulus to each other, I suspect in the role of equal partners at least until *BPPL* (although this may not be a widely accepted view).[26]

Their major objective in the 1920s was to elaborate upon their earlier discussions of trade cycle theory; more specifically they were attempting to integrate interest rate theory and saving/investment analysis into the theory of industrial fluctuation. For Robertson the focus of his work was upon the role of banks in the cycle; this reflected what he saw as an overemphasis upon the importance of monetary forces in the trade cycle: 'far more weight must be attached than it is now fashionable to attach to certain real, as opposed to monetary or psychological, causes of fluctuation'.[27] In this he was arguing against the extreme position of Hawtrey ('the trade cycle is a purely monetary phenomenon')[28] and the less extreme view of Keynes's *TMR* that the initial disturbance in the price level may be the result of non monetary causes but that it should be counteracted via monetary policy.[29]

Keynes and Robertson worked very closely on four books in this period. *Money, TMR, BPPL* and *TM*; none appeared under joint authorship though clearly the published acknowledgements and correspondence indicate the tremendous debt they owed to each other in their respective publications.[30] A typical example of this joint effort can be gained by a more thorough examination of *BPPL*. This will also serve as a prelude to establishing why their later conflicts over theory were so painful, since much of Robertson's displeasure over the drafts of the *GT* stem from their departure from the approach of *BPPL*.

Alongside the *Study, BPPL* ranks as Robertson's most important contribution to economic theory. Its publication followed long correspondence between Keynes and Robertson which by May 1925 had resulted in almost total agreement on its contents.[31] In the preface Robertson wrote: 'I have had so many discussions with Mr J. M. Keynes on the subject matters of chapters V and VI and have rewritten them so drastically at his suggestion, that I think neither of us now knows how much of the ideas therein contained is his and how much is mine;.[32] That Keynes accepted the fundamental arguments within *BPPL* is confirmed by correspondence. Keynes wrote: 'I like this latest version though God knows it is concise'.[33] He regarded Chapter V as 'splendid – most new and important. I think it is substantially right and at last I have no material criticism. It is the kernel and ideal essence of the book'.[34]

It is instructive to examine what Keynes was agreeing with in *BPPL*. The major objective of *BPPL*, as the title suggest, was to formulate guide lines for banking policy over the course of the cycle, particularly in relation to the desired behaviour of the price level. The real over-investment theory of the *Study* was the acceptable starting point; *BPPL* sought to develop cycle theory by establishing the role of monetary

forces in exaggerating cyclical movements and consequently the function of banking policy in avoiding such inappropriate fluctuations. Its
approach was in marked contrast with the *GT*. Robertson employed
dynamic analysis, a step-by-step approach. He believed that it was
imperative to recognise the time lags which existed in the relationships
between economic variables; indeed he saw the differences portrayed in
time lags in competing theories as often the major expression of differences between theories.[35] The application of 'period analysis' in *BPPL*
led Robertson to present a very complex view of the nature of savings
over the cycle. Saving was disaggregated; it did not consist merely of
voluntary savings; indeed Robertson was to incorporate his own terminology. Saving became 'lacking', this could be automatic or induced,
long or short; he then talked of 'splashing' and also of 'stinting' which
again had their own subdivisions, and so the Robertsonian concept
of saving emerged.[36] Saving was, in turn, related to the behaviour of
the price level, the monetary system and the finance of investment.

What all this amounted to was a dynamic theory of forced saving, an
extension of the type of theory which had been propounded before in
'classical' literature.[37] It had however one special ingredient, a remarkable one which, in fact, was contributed by Keynes . This was a concept
of 'induced lacking'.[38] The idea that those on fixed incomes may be
'forced' to save in a situation where prices were rising was not new in
1926. That individuals may be 'induced' to save was however given
much greater emphasis in *BPPL* than in previous work.

In defining induced lacking Robertson wrote:

> induced lacking occurs when, the same process that imposes auto-
> matic lacking on certain people having also reduced the real value of
> their money stocks, these people hold off the market, and refrain
> from consuming the full value of their current output, in order to bring
> the real value of their money stocks up again to what they regard as
> an appropriate level.[39]

In an appendix Robertson also attempts to employ induced lacking in an
attempt at 'stability analysis'. Surprisingly it was Keynes who prompted
Robertson to recognise this real balance effect. In May 1925 he wrote
of a situation in which money supply and prices were increasing:

no position of equilibrium can be reached until someone is induced to replenish his hoard, i.e., to do *some new* hoarding out of current income. It is only when this occurs that new short lacking is provided.

This inducement to effect new hoarding comes about, in general, in one of three ways:

1.   The real deposits of the public may fall to a highly inconvenient low proportion of their real income, so that they prefer to do new hoarding so as to raise them, rather than to maintain their current expenditure at its previous level.
2.   Inflation may effect a redistribution of current real income into the hands of people whose incentive and ability to hoard is greater than those from whose it is taken.
3.   A higher bank rate may increase the incentive to hoard.[40]

The first bears a strong resemblance to the real balance effect. In the same letter Keynes also writes on the redistributional effects of inflation and the effects on inflationary expectations of an increase in money supply and prices. Both arguments were subsequently utilized by Robertson in *BPPL*.

To summarize, without doubt Keynes and Robertson were almost as one over the contents of *BPPL*. Keynes clearly had a major share of the credit for its originality. As such Keynes made no objection to its dynamic approach, he was happy to accept its theory of forced saving and indeed was prepared to assist in its elaboration. He made no fundamental criticisms of the disaggregated nature of Robertson's saving analysis, nor of Robertson's persistent classification of fluctuations into those which were appropriate and those which were inappropriate; that appropriate fluctuation (continuous disequilibrium?) was desirable in the interests of economic progress remained a central feature of *BPPL* as it was in the *Study*.

Keynes had begun *TM* in 1924, and its subsequent drafts still exhibited much of the analysis of *BPPL* as late as August 1929, when Keynes was still content to incorporate the forced saving thesis in a draft of Chapter 23.[41] However, it was omitted from the published version which appeared in 1930. This about-turn by Keynes brought with it differences with Robertson in the definitions of savings and investment, in the nature of saving over the cycle and ultimately in the appropriate banking policy. *TM* was the beginning of totally different approaches of Robertson and Keynes to the analysis of economic fluctuations. They had gone forward together throughout the 1920s, but now their paths were to diverge, not so much on policy issues but on the theoretical justification of the policies which they both advocated.

The partial breakdown in their working relationship was disguised by their correspondence. Keynes thought that *TM* would 'get through the criticisms of Robertson . . . without serious damage' and indeed believed that *TM* 'owes a great deal to him'.[42] Robertson described *TM* as 'marvellously full of new meat . . . I think the whole book VII, most of which is new to me, splendid'.[43] But at the same time he was resistant to large parts of it.[44] Much later he attacked Keynes for his conformity with the traditional approach in *TM*, particularly on the question of monetary stabilisation. (He believed that Keynes was calling for price stabilisation.) In *BPPL* he had proposed that banking policy might promote instability in the price level in order to facilitate the creation of credit necessary to finance both working and fixed capital over the trade cycle.

Although both *BPPL* and *TM* recognise the inequality of saving and investment over the course of the cycle, Robertson did not see excessive saving as a cause, but a symptom of depression.[45] The debate in the *Economic Journal* which followed the publication of *TM* has the outward appearance of a dispute over the definitions of saving and investment. It was, however, much more fundamental than this. Robertson was unhappy that Keynes had failed to evolve the view of the economic system he had put forward in *BPPL*, a discontent which was to grow with the drafts of the *GT*.

WORKING OUT THE GENERAL THEORY AND AFTER: UNPRODUCTIVE COLLABORATION?

The period from 1931 onwards has justifiably gained most attention from historians of Keynesians economic thought in recent years. It would be fruitless simply to reiterate what has gone before; this section therefore makes a general comment on the working relationship of Keynes and Robertson in this period and secondly attempts to explain why Robertson was so critical of the *GT*.

The current literature reveals two popular interpretations of the period 1931–6. D. Patinkin concludes from his study of Keynes's writing of the *GT* that: 'the received version of the transition from the *Treatise* to the *General Theory* assigned too large a role to the discussions of the "Cambridge Circus", and correspondingly too small a one to the criticisms of such individuals as Hawtrey, Robertson and even Hayek'.[46] The received version, of course, is associated with the excellent work of D. Moggridge who has been largely responsible for collecting and editing Keynes's papers and correspondence. Moggridge writes:

Ralph Hawtrey and Dennis Robertson were even further outside the inner circle (Cambridge Circus). Although their comments may have been formally correct on occasion, they appear to have had little effect on the final product, except in cases where they either echoed points raised by others in close sympathy with the whole exercise or where Kahn and Joan Robinson . . . commended their criticisms to Keynes.[47]

As far as Robertson is concerned, my inclination is towards Moggridge's interpretation of this period. Robertson only attended, at most, one meeting of the Cambridge 'circus'. He was the first to see drafts of the *GT* outside of the 'circus' but in response to them he complained to Keynes: 'a large part of your theoretical structure is still to me almost complete mumbo-jumbo!'[48] Offended by this remark and upset by critical comment from Robertson on the drafts, in March 1935 Keynes broke off the debate with Robertson and only minor correspondence then took place between them. It is a fair interpretation therefore that during this period Robertson had very little of a positive nature to offer Keynes for the *GT*.

There is however a further important point to be made. Keynes had been moving towards the *GT* through *TMR*, *BPPL* and *TM*; admittedly the final contents of the *GT* had been worked out from 1931–5, but the pre-1931 period was also important in providing Keynes with a foundation from which to build this *GT*. The contention here is that Robertson was as influential as anyone in creating that foundation. Keynes, as we saw earlier, regarded Robertson as his parent leading him from the classical fold. Together they had conducted their debate in the 1920s in terms of saving and investment, although the definitions employed of saving and investment differed significantly from those of the *GT*. Keynes was already, by 1931, prepared to recognise the possible inequality of saving and investment over the cycle; he had been exposed to Robertson's belief in public spending policies as a cure for unemployment and this followed logically from Robertson's view of a deficiency in demand for capital goods as a cause of depression. Robertson also had continuously stressed the importance of investment in the economic system and the causes of its volatility as the source of macroeconomic fluctuation. Neither by 1931 had any great respect for Say's Law. The *GT* was also to lay stress upon investment, although through the multiplier process. The Cambridge School, with Robertson as a leading member, had also conducted its analysis of monetary factors in terms of the real cash balance approach. It preferred to look at the demand for money rather than 'money on the wing'. Keynes also chose this approach in the liquidity preference theory. Hence Keynes did depart from the 'classical' fold in the *GT*, but he was already being encouraged to do so before 1931 by Robertson (and also by R. G. Hawtrey) and this clearly had its implications for the writing of the *GT*. Given this encouragement by Robertson to rebel against the 'classical' approach, one may be surprised by his negative reaction to the *GT*. There are however two major reasons for this:

(1)   Keynes was keen to present the *GT* as a revolution in economic thought; Robertson had always viewed his own work as evolving from the work of Cambridge economists, past and present. Like many within Cambridge he believed that 'it's all in Marshall' and always saw his work on industrial fluctuation as extending theories within the Cambridge School. He believed that Keynes had given too little credit to the work of Marshall and Pigou in influencing the *GT* and was far too content in being critical of what had gone before. Robertson always upheld that there was an element of truth in all theories and that they should not be dismissed too lightly. He gave considerable effort to showing that substantial pieces in the *GT* could be traced back to classical and Cambridge writings. Keynes was upset by this and accused

Robertson of always retreating to his mother's womb (the 'Cambridge School') while he had been able to shake himself free of it.

(2)   Probably of more weight than (1), Robertson was deeply disappointed with the *GT* because it did not evolve out of their joint work in the 1920s, particularly *BPPL*. He clearly felt that his own approach in *BPPL* was superior to that of the *GT*. He later wrote: 'not only did Keynes fail to acknowledge what had gone before, but many aspects of his work which had not gone before represented erroneous argument rather than economic truth'.[49] The *GT* was too simplistic in approach. Robertson objected to its use of comparative statics and also its failure to disaggregate. His attack upon the multiplier process was typical of his view of the *GT* through the eyes of *BPPL*. The instantaneous equilibrium it brought about, the equality of investment and voluntary saving, disguised for Robertson the true nature of the economic system. It ignored the time lags which were apparent in the real world; it failed to take account of the accelerator; and above all it treated the finance of investment via voluntary saving as unproblematical. In this manner the *GT* dispensed with much of the analysis of *BPPL* which had been primarily concerned with the complexities of the saving process and the problem of providing finance for investment over the trade cycle.

But this was for Keynes the advantage of *GT*; he had regarded *BPPL* as too complex and far too difficult to understand.[50] The *GT* was an attempt to present a view of the functioning of the macroeconomic system which could be understood by a larger audience. Robertson had never been in a position where *BPPL* had been widely accepted. Despite its relevance, its contents defied the understanding of the vast majority of its readers.

SOME CONCLUSIONS

The paper has attempted to view the working relationship between Keynes and Robertson before 1940 as three distinct phases. In so doing it has avoided the inclination to concentrate upon the later period during the writing of the *GT*. Clearly the relationship between these two eminent economists was much closer not only for 1910–15 but more importantly for the 1920s than it was in the 1930s. It has attempted to demonstrate the existence of a much longer gestation period for the *GT* than one gathers from contemporary literature. While not suggesting that the pre-1931 period deserves equal treatment, it was nevertheless productive in carrying economics forward beyond the classical system and there were few economists more pioneering in this respect than Keynes and Robertson.

ACKNOWLEDGEMENTS

I would like to thank S. R. Dennison and Professor T. Cate for assistance on this paper. I am also grateful to the Wincott Foundation, the British Academy and the Economic and Social Research Council for providing grants to support my research on Sir D. H. Robertson. The paper was presented at the History of Economics Society Conference at George Mason University, April 1985.

NOTES

1. J. M. Keynes, *The General Theory of Employment, Interest and Money* (London: Macmillan, 1936).
2. D. H. Robertson, *Banking Policy and the Price Level* (London: P. S. King and Son Ltd, 1926).
3. J. M. Keynes, *The Treaties on Money* (London: Macmillan, 1930).
4. J. R. Hicks, 'The Monetary Theory of D. H. Robertson', *Economica*, New Series, 9–10 February 1942, p. 55.
5. D. H. Robertson, *Money* (London: Nisbet and Co. 1922).
6. J. M. Keynes, *The Tract on Monetary Reform* (London: Macmillan, 1923).
7. R. F. Harrod, *The Life of John Maynard Keynes* (London: Macmillan, 1951) Ch. XIII.
8. Letter from Professor S. R. Dennison to the author, 16 March 1985.
9. D. H. Robertson, *A Study of Industrial Fluctuation* (London: P. S. King and Son Ltd, 1915).
10. J. M. Keynes, *The Collected Writings of J. M. Keynes*, vol. XIII (London: Macmillan, for the Royal Economic Society, 1973) p. 1.
11. Ibid., p. 1.
12. The precise title was: 'How Far are Bankers Responsible for the Alternatives of Crisis and Depression? (J. M. Keynes, (1973), *op. cit.*, p. 2)

13. J. M. Keynes, (1973), *op. cit.*, p. 9
14. D. H. Robertson, (1915), *op. cit.*, p. xx.
15. M. Labordère, 'Autour de la Crisis Americaine de 1907', *Revue de Paris*, 1 February 1908.
16. W. Mitchell, *Business Cycles: The Problem and its Setting* (New York: Burt Franklin, 1913).
17. D. H. Robertson, (1915), *op. cit.*, p. 171.
18. Ibid., p. 171.
19. Ibid., pt II, Ch. IV.
20. P. Lambert, 'The Evolution of Keynes's Thought from the *Treatise on Money* to the *General Theory*', *Annals of Public and Cooperative Economy*, 1969, pp. 1–21.
21. J. M. Keynes, *The Collected Writings of John Maynard Keynes*, vol. XIV (London: Macmillan, for the Royal Economic Society, 1973) p. 202.
22. D. H. Robertson, (1915), *op. cit.*, p. 254.
23. D. H. Robertson, (1915), *op. cit.*, 1948 edition, p. ix.
24. D. Moggridge and S. Howson, 'Keynes on Monetary Policy 1910–46', *Oxford Economic Papers*, 26 (2) July 1974, pp. 227–34.
25. An address by D. H. Robertson to the Conference of Economics Teachers, Oxford, 4 January 1947 entitled 'The Frontiers of Economic Thought', unpublished. The brackets are mine.
26. J. Leith and D. Patinkin, *Keynes, Cambridge and the General Theory* (London: Macmillan, 1977).
27. D. H. Robertson, (1926), *op. cit.*, p. 1.
28. R. G. Hawtrey, *Monetary Reconstruction* (London: Longmans, 1919) p. 141.
29. J. M. Keynes, (1923), *op. cit.*, p. 38.
30. J. R. Presley, *Robertsonian Economics* (London: Macmillan, 1978) Part II.
31. The only minor difference by May 1925 was over real hoarding and new short lacking, which Keynes regarded as identical. Robertson in fact accepted Keynes's standpoint in the published version of *BPPL* (J. M. Keynes, 1973, p. 38).
32. D. H. Robertson, (1926), *op. cit.*, p. 5.
33. J. M. Keynes, (1973), *op. cit.*, p. 39.
34. Ibid., p.40.
35. J. R. Presley, *op. cit.*, p. 154.
36. Ibid., Part II.
37. B. Corry, *Money, Saving and Investment in English Economics 1800–50* (London: Macmillan, 1952).
38. J. R. Presley, 'Keynes and the Real Balance Effect', *Manchester School*, Spring 1986.
39. D. H. Robertson, 1926), *op. cit.*, p. 61.
40. J. M. Keynes, (1973), *op. cit.*, pp. 36–7.

41. Ibid., pp. 104–8.
42. J. M. Keynes, *The Collected Writings of John Maynard Keynes*, vol. XIX (London: Macmillan, 1979 for the Royal Economic Society) p. 2.
43. J. M. Keynes, (1973), *op. cit.*, p. 202.
44. Ibid., pp. 21–2.
45. D. H. Robertson, 'Industrial Fluctuation and the Natural Rate of Interest', *Economic Journal*, December 1934, pp. 650–6.
46. J. Leith and D. Patinkin, *op. cit.*, p. 6.
47. Ibid., p. 68.
48. J. M. Keynes, (1973), *op. cit.*, p. 506.
49. Letter from D. H. Robertson to Professor T. Wilson, dated 31 October 1953.
50. J. M. Keynes, (1973), *op. cit.*, pp. 39–40.

6 Professor Robertson On Effective Demand And The Trade Cycle

Thomas Wilson

To attempt a survey of Professor Robertson's views on effective demand and the trade cycle, is a task which is extremely difficult, and perhaps impossible, to carry out satisfactorily. Four books by Professor Robertson have appeared since the end of the war, but three of these are new editions of earlier works to which only a small amount of new writing has been added. It is true that his new writing – in the form of two additional chapters in *Money* (1948), and new introductions to *A Study of Industrial Fluctuation* (1948), and to *Banking Policy and the Price Level* (1949)[1] raises a host of intricate and important issues that deserve the closest attention; but there is no detailed positive statement of the position Professor Robertson would now adopt and his additions consist in the main of criticism of Keynesian economics and a vindication of earlier views on these matters. The post-war essays now brought together in the fourth volume, *Utility and All That* (1952), are also predominantly critical and do not include a systematic presentation of his own views on some of the topics with which we must deal.

This is unfortunate, although we must be careful not to imply a question-begging way that his earlier theories, as set out in the original parts of these new editions and in some of the *Essays in Monetary Theory*, are so badly out of date as to be in need of drastic revision. 'After so many years', writes Professor Fellner[2] 'a surprisingly small part of Robertsonian's early contribution is outmoded in the sense that a problem with which it is concerned seems to have lost its significance, or in the sense that a statement is clearly less adequate than later statements of other authors on the same subject'. Large parts of these pioneering works seem modern even to-day, and some other parts that do not seem so modern are perhaps none the worse for that! For example, his treatment of investment deserves to be studied as a much-needed corrective to some modern tendencies. So much must be conceded, but we must also assume that in certain respects he would now modify his theories, and it is here that we feel a certain lack of guidance.

Faced with this difficulty, we shall have to follow an indirect path in the hope that it will lead us, if not all the way to the correct destination at least some distance in the right direction; it is a long path, and a somewhat rough one, for it runs through Professor Robertson's prolonged dispute with Keynes. Their famous controversy could not, it is true, be avoided, even if we had some more detailed account of Professor Robertson's views, but without the latter it must be given a more central position than might otherwise seem appropriate; for we must try to extract from his critical survey of Keynesian ideas some inferences about the extent to which the earlier Robertsonian theories might now be revised if their author were to set himself that task.

In order to assess the outcome of such a battle of giants one would need not merely a detailed knowledge of the extensive literature but also a sense of perspective which is very difficult for a member of my generation to acquire. For we began our study of these matters in the exciting years of the Keynesian Revolution, and whether we supported it or opposed it – or merely tried to keep out of harm's way – our minds were so occupied with the events of the time that, although the dust of the fighting has now begun to clear a little, it is still far from easy either to understand the *ancien regime* or to form a balanced judgement about the Revolution which established the New Economics. I can only say that to my mind much of Professor Robertson's criticism seems unanswerable, provided each point is examined in detail and to some extent in isolation; but I am not so convinced that he does full justice to the more positive achievements of the *General Theory*, or that he is always fully successful in avoiding the temptation to vindicate what went before by reference to passages in the earlier literature which may be isolated and not altogether characteristic. Professor Hicks once said of Keynes that he was 'the most Impressionist' of all great economists, and went on to observe that Professor Robertson's criticisms 'sometimes remind me of a man examining a Seurat with a microscope and denouncing the ugly shapes of the individual dots'.[3] There may be an element of truth in this remark about some of Professor Robertson's comments; but it would scarcely apply to all of them, and, in any case,

I suppose it is always open to Professor Robertson to reply that it was part of Keynes's job as a professional economist to deal faithfully with detail instead of – in Ruskin's phrase – 'flinging a pot of paint in the public's face'.

The second of the chapters now added to *Money* bears the title 'Problem of Words, Thought and Action', and everyone who is familiar with the literature will be well aware of the trouble the Words have caused. It was Keynes who was largely responsible for starting the uproar, and it is, I think, undeniable that most of what Keynes said in the *General Theory* could have been put in terms which would have been more familiar and more acceptable to many of his colleagues. But that is not the whole of the story. The instinct that led him to adopt a different course may have been a sound one because a major change of emphasis can be achieved only with difficulty if the argument is couched in language which, by long usage and association, evokes responses now held to be undesirable; both author and reader will slip less readily into their old habits of thought if the jargon is new. Keynes appears to have sensed this. In discussing Keynes's attitude to the classical economists, Mr Harrod observes 'He felt he would get nowhere if he did not raise the dust'.[4] It is certainly doubtful whether he would otherwise have eradicated so completely what was left of the Treasury View and smothered so utterly the partially discredited but obstinately recurrent protest that thriftiness can never be excessive. To-day the unsatisfactory condition of the theory of the firm confronts us with a problem in the choice of terminology so analogous to that confronting Keynes that we can, perhaps, sympathise more readily with the course he adopted. It is at least arguable that on balance Keynes was right to change the language as well as the emphasis; but it is clear that the price he had to pay was heavy. His somewhat brusque rejection of so much of the earlier work on the subject appeared unreasonable and gave rise to protracted and somewhat unprofitable controversies. Worse still, he came near to confusing his own mind with some of his innovations. For this reason it is not surprising that Professor Robertson should have felt obliged to reply to the Keynesian onslaught in a long series of articles and reviews; to do so was a necessary and important task. But I am inclined to suspect that the polemical literature, both Keynesian, and Robertsonian, leaves an exaggerated impression of the differences between their respective theories, at all events we must try to see how much real disagreement is left when the terminological difficulties are disposed of. That there is real disagreement is undeniable, but its detection is only part of our task. We may note those innovations in Keynesian theory that Professor Robertson cannot fully accept, but we shall find it more difficult to indicate those he does accept. How far would he now revise his earlier theory in the light of the New Economics? Without more positive statements from Professor Robertson, I can only speculate – and hopefully trail my coat.

I

The defects of Keynes's theory of the rate of interest have engaged Professor Robertson's attention for many years – too much so, perhaps, because he had tended to neglect his own vastly important theory of the connection between economic progress and the trade cycle. As Professor Hicks has observed, the controversy has been, at least in part, a bogus one,[5] for it is not difficult to reconcile the proposition that the rate of interest is determined by the demand for loanable funds and their supply with the proposition that it depends upon liquidity preference and the amount of money. In my view, Keynes's new approach was in this case unfortunate. First, it is easier, I suspect, to go behind broad statements and examine in detail the working of the financial institutions if the analysis is conducted in terms of loanable funds. Secondly, it seems probable that, if Keynes had adopted the older approach, he would have escaped the temptation to suggest that changes in savings and investment could have no direct effect on the rate of interest; by conceding their *possible* influence while maintaining that the other constituents of loanable funds were *in fact* more important, he might have avoided much unnecessary controversy from the outset. It would then have been clear that Keynes was making an empirical generalisation, backed by his own intimate knowledge of the capital market, rather than performing some kind of analytical conjuring trick. His generalisation that 'speculative' purchases and sales were a dominating determinant of security prices would have been contrasted at once with the older view that changes connected with idle balances were relatively unimportant, and although there would still, no doubt, have been controversy, it would have been directed to the real point at issue the interpretation of the facts.[6] If the argument so far is accepted, are there any basic differences between Professor Robertson's views and the expurgated Keynesian theory I have tried to suggest?

It seems almost unnecessary to say that Professor Robertson has never implied that savings and investment are the only two constituents of loanable funds that matter.[7] He has observed, it is true, that in his opinion productivity and thrift are likely to be the more important factors in the long run,[8] but he has always recognised that, in the short run at least, changes in the total amount of money together with hoarding or dishoarding may exert a major influence. Indeed, if this were not so, the divergences between savings and investment that are basic to the Robertsonian theory could not occur. The differences between Robertson and Keynes were therefore much less fundamental than those which separated both of them from the defenders of Say's Law.

Paradoxically, the importance of hoarding and dishoarding received very much greater emphasis in the *General Theory* than it had done before. The paradox lies in Keynes's reluctant and dubious use of the term 'hoarding'.[9] In a famous passage he says that 'it is impossible for the actual amount of hoarding to change as a result of decisions on the part of the public, so long as we mean by "hoarding" the actual holding of cash. For the amount of hoarding must be equal to the quantity of money'.[10] It may be, as Professor Villard suggests, that the difficulty arose because 'the instantaneous approach of the *General Theory* avoids as far as possible specific reference to time periods, while "hoarding" in its usual meaning must have a time dimension'.[11]

This may be part of the explanation, but to my mind it seems natural, in working out the Keynesian theory, to regard as the principal form of hoarding (or dishoarding) those changes in M_2 balances on which his theory of the rate of interest partly depends. If, for example, business obtains additional funds for expansion because, liquidity preference being what it is, securities are bought out of M_2 balances with a corresponding increase in M_1 balances, 'dishoarding' in the older sense of the term has occurred.[12] Professor Robertson, for his part, has little difficulty in showing that 'the fallacy of hoarding' is not a fallacy after all. He defines 'hoarding' as 'a decrease in the income velocity of circulation of money';[13] and if this is taken to mean a fall in the ratio of Y to M_1 *plus* M_2,[14] it is not easy to see why there should be any unbridgeable gap at this point between the Robertsonian and the Keynesian theories.

It may be that Keynes laid too much emphasis on the 'speculative' purchase and sale of securities: apart from the possibility that productivity and thrift may have some direct influence, a good deal more needs to be said about the behaviour of the banks.[15] But would Professor Robertson for his part not be prepared to concede that the factors on which the theory of liquidity preference lays a too exclusive emphasis had previously been, if not ignored, at all events too little stressed by most economists? Would he not agree that Keynes was justified in underlining the fact that liquidity preference may make it impossible in bad times to lower the long-term rate of interest below what is considered a 'safe' level? After all Keynes was really taking up a point made by Professor Robertson himself before the Macmillan Committee in 1930, although, as Professor Robertson admits, he had failed to carry general conviction – partly because of Keynes's own 'sturdy Johnsonian classicism!'[16] Years later, it was Keynes, with his classicism now abandoned, who successfully performed the task of persuasion. Here, as so often in studying the controversy provoked by the *General Theory*, one feels that Professor Robertson is not so much denying the significance of the factors stressed by Keynes but rather protesting that these factors, to which he himself had previously tried to call attention, are not the only ones that have to be taken into account.

In this connection Keynes surely made a real contribution by stimulating the study of the considerations that may lead people to hoard or dishoard. 'Where I suspect there is still work to be done', wrote Professor Robertson himself in his review of the *Treatise*, 'is in clearing up the nature of the forces which let the spirit of hoarding loose'. This is what Keynes sought to do when he emphasised that uncertainty about the future of security prices was a reason for holding cash. His treatment of the matter may not have been fully satisfactory, and there was some trouble with 'boot straps'; but progress had been made and an impetus had been given to further study. There is still 'work to be done', and it is difficult work because the facts are so elusive. We need not expect agreement to be reached for an indefinite period, but there is little sign of a divergence so fundamental to imply radically different views about the causes of monetary instability.

Before leaving the topic of hoarding it may be as well as to make clear that, in attempting to reach a compromise in the use of terms, it has not been implied that the velocity of circulation varies only with changes in M_1 balances relatively to M_2 balances. The ratio between M_1 balances and the monetary value of output should not be regarded as altogether rigid, and the variations that take place can have a direct effect on demand, not an indirect effect transmitted through the rate of interest.[17] The speculative balances themselves may be held not only with an eye to future security prices; possible fluctuations in the prices of commodities may also afford a stimulus to become more or less liquid, and we must make some provision for balances built up out of forced savings during a period of suppressed inflation. The Keynesian division into M_1 and M_2 balances has been a very helpful one, but there is a need for some modifications and for a certain amount of tidying up.

II

A sufficient measure of agreement has not been reached about the definitions of saving and investment to allow us to dispose fairly quickly of the controversy to which the *General Theory* gave rise. There is a flat inconsistency in that work between the 'straightforward book-keeping usage',[18] which implies necessary equality between savings and invest-ment, and the proposition that the two are brought into equality by a fluctuation in income.[19] This, as Professor Robertson reminds us, is about as sensible as to define an elephant's trunk and its proboscis in identical terms, and then 'to go to explain the profound biological forces which tend to adjust the size of the trunk to the size of the proboscis'.[20] It is sometimes held that Keynes can be defended against the charge of formal inconsistency on the grounds that in his model lags were assumed to be zero; but this will not do. Keynes refers to output lags, and it is not neglect of them but an irrelevant reversion to the *ex post* definitions which makes him nevertheless maintain that 'the logical theory of the multiplier . . . holds good continuously, without time-lag, at all moments of time' (*General Theory*, p. 122). Thus any such attempt to justify his use of definitions at the expense of his sense of realism is likely to encounter difficulties. Mr Harry Johnson made an attempt of this kind: 'The Keynesian theory', he writes, '. . . is a static theory; it is not concerned with the succession of changing equilibrium positions'.[21] Now in a situation of equilibrium *ex ante* saving and investment will be equal as well as *ex post* saving and investment, and Mr Johnson assures us that 'no difficulty arises from the Keynesian definition if a strictly static form of argument is adhered to; for then only positions of simultaneous equilibrium of all the variables are involved". This is so, but as a defence of Keynes's exposition it is unconvincing. All the variables may be equal in positions of equilibrium, but that does not obliterate the distinction that Keynes failed to draw between the *ex post* and the *ex ante*. Admittedly, the confusion in Keynes's mind may have been less serious than Professor Robertson's criticism implies: Keynes seems in places on the very verge of drawing this distinction. The fact remains that he did not do so, and his work remains, therefore, open to valid criticism. Is it not, perhaps, unfortunate that some Keynesians have been reluctant to concede as much and have thus tended to prolong the controversy?

Professor Robertson relates to-day's consumption to yesterday's income, but it must not be inferred from this that he assumes any simple and constant relationship between the two. Although he has not denied that income is one of the determinants of consumption, he has been at some pains to emphasise the importance of other factors, such as changes in the distribution of income and variations in the liquid reserves held by consumers. The importance of these complicating factors is now more generally recognised, and a good deal of the more recent work on fluctuations in consumption can be regarded – though this is rarely done – as a vindication of Professor Robertson's views. The fall in the propensity to consume during a cyclical upswing is clearly attributable to some other important factors as well as to the rise in real income, and it is therefore unwise to predict, on the strength of cyclical experience, that consumption will fall relatively to real income over a longer period as a community grows wealthier. To take one of these other factors: the shift to profits during an upswing tends to pull down the proportion of income consumed, but over the trend there may be no sustained tendency for the distribution of income to change in this way.[22] By allowing for such complications – including, of course, those discussed by Duesenberry[23] – the contrast between the cyclical and secular behaviour of the propensity to consume can be largely explained. The implications are not altogether favourable for the Keynesian theory of long-term stagnation, but the Robertsonian sequence analysis is not in any way invalidated. Its validity does not depend upon there being any simple functional relationship between yesterday's income and to-day's consumption; nor does it depend upon there being a lengthy interval of time between the receipt of income and its expenditure. His sequence analysis should rather be regarded as a way of indicating that saving is *attempted* saving, not simply the total sums that happen not to be spent. The latter may exceed or fall short of attempted savings if the economy is not in equilibrium, and a mere equality between not-spending and actual investment is no indication of stability. Although his analysis differs in some respects from that of the Swedes, there is an obvious family resemblance.

The lag between the receipt of income and its expenditure has come to be known as the 'Robertson Lag', and this would be reasonable enough if it were not implied at the same time that Professor Robertson has neglected other lags. Professor Metzler, in an otherwise valuable and instructive essay, has gone so far as to say explicitly that: 'Robertson . . . assumes that consumers' expenditure lags behind income, and that within a given expenditure period, output responds immediately to a change in sales'.[24] This is surely an odd thing to say about the author of *A Study of Industrial Fluctuation* where Aftalion's *Gestation Period* is discussed at length in both analytical and statistical terms. It must be conceded that, in his later writings, rather less attention is given to the *Gestation Period*, but it is by no means ignored. One of the limitations of the usual models of the multiplier is that changes in consumers' expenditure and changes in the output of consumers' good are treated as though they were a single act, but Professor Robertson must not have this assumption attributed to *him*.[25]

Although the controversy about saving and investment has now been fairly well cleared up, Professor Robertson, for his part, seems inclined to the view that the echoes of the original confusion remained, and may, conceivably have influenced policy in the post-war period. Thus he quotes the following statement by Lord Beveridge: 'capital expenditure itself brings into existence the very savings necessary to finance it'. 'Now does not that sentence,' asks Professor Robertson, 'cry out for completion in some such words as these – and can never therefore be carried out on an excessive scale?'[26] Although this passage in Beveridge's work[27] is unfortunately expressed and contains some dubious remarks about the rate of interest, I do not think it could be shown that he, or indeed any competent Keynesian, has ever been so preoccupied with the *ex post* identity as to apply the argument without reference to the amount of unused resources,[28] but at a less sophisticated – though not unimportant – level of discussion, the error may well be encountered. Ideas tend to lose their subtlety in the process of becoming more generally accepted, and some of Keynes's remarks, half-understood and applied in a manner that would have shocked their author, may have tended in recent years to undermine the traditional maxims that used to impose some restraint on extravagance in public expenditure. As for Lord Beveridge, his real error lay not so much in giving universal application to the proposition quoted above as in assuming that conditions after the war would shortly be such as to make it relevant. In this he was not alone; most of us made the same mistake.

III

The Theory of the Multiplier, as presented in the *General Theory*, suffered from Keynes's failure to distinguish between attempted saving and investment and actual saving, and investment. (The effect of this faulty treatment can still be seen in the improper identification of the relationship between investment and income, as measured by the statisticians, with the Multiplier.) But the error can be corrected and the theory expounded, as Professor Robertson himself has shown,[29] in a form which, whatever its limitations, is at least free from this internal inconsistency. That the theory has its limitations is undeniable, but is it really nothing more than 'a little piece of algebra which serves in many expositions as a magic carpet to waft us from one platform to the next'? It is long past the time that people began to speak irreverently about the multiplier, but apart from the need at the moment for a certain amount of debunking, is this a fair comment? And is the Propensity to Consume nothing more than 'a potentially useful little brick'?[30]

The verdict on the Theory of the Multiplier will largely depend upon whether the expression is interpreted in a narrow sense to mean 'the little piece of algebra' or more broadly to cover some general considerations of which 'the little piece of algebra' is merely a special example. The simple algebraic model is based on a number of limiting assumptions – constancy in the marginal propensity to consume, complete elasticity in the supply of funds, complete elasticity in the supply of consumer's goods, zero elasticity of expectations, no induced investment, no secondary effects on public finance and no effect on foreign trade. In this form the theory is open to at least as much criticism as the more mechanistic versions of the Acceleration Principle, and it is a little odd that some of those who have poured scorn on the latter are still prepared to treat the former with apparently undiminished respect. Both theories, however, can be presented less rigidly and in more general terms, and both are then of major importance. That of the Multiplier has served to attract attention to considerations, which, if not entirely ignored, were inadequately appreciated before its appearance: that, at a time when large numbers are out of work, the beneficial effect on employment of a rise in investment will not be confined to the industries making capital goods; that, if there are idle resources, consumption and investment are likely to move in the same direction instead of being alternatives as the earlier theories, which usually started with the initial assumption of full employment, were wont to suggest; that the marginal propensity to consume, whether constant or not, will be *one* of the major determinants of the magnitude of the subsequent change in income. It is in some such general sense that Professor Robertson himself seems to be using the term when he refers, in the new introduction to *Industrial Fluctuation*, to the 'multiplier effects' in Marshall's account of a trade depression.[31] Moreover, it should be observed, in fairness, that in Professor Kahn's original exposition a great deal of attention was devoted to some limitations of 'the little piece of algebra', and Keynes himself had some qualifying remarks to make. It is also true that account was quickly taken of the secondary changes in Investment that a multiplier expansion may induce. 'Dogs wag tails, as well as tails dogs',[32] but the 'double wag' was one of the main features of Mr Harrod's *Trade Cycle* which followed the *General Theory* after a very short interval.

Professor Robertson has shown how satisfactorily his own period analysis can be used to expound the Theory of the Multiplier, although his object in doing so was to criticise. In view of their protracted controversy, it is ironical to reflect that Keynes, for his part, might well have escaped the confusion into which he fell if he had adopted this technique and used it to express ideas which were probably more important *in the thirties* than those contained in most of Professor Robertson's own models. With the wisdom that comes after the event, one cannot help feeling that the most natural and obvious development of Professor Robertson's technique was to introduce various assumptions about the marginal propensity to consume; Keynes does not appear to have seen this, and Professor Robertson himself took this further step only after the publication of the *General Theory* – and without any obvious enthusiasm.[33] In the new Preface to *Banking Policy and the Price Level* he now observes that, 'While Keynes must at the time have understood and acquiesced in my step-by-step method, it is evident that it never, so to speak, got under his skin''. Admittedly the persuasiveness of Robertson's earlier work was greatly weakened by what he now calls his 'somewhat *outré* technical terms'; but the idea of a period analysis could have been adopted without taking over all those terms.

IV

We have referred above to Professor Robertson's preoccupation in most of his writings with inflationary expansions, and it is not surprising that he should now complain about the comparative neglect of price changes in much of the Keynesian literature. In particular, he condemns Mrs Robinson's suggestion that there should be 'two separate compartments of thought, one a theory of money proper and the other a theory of output or employment'.[34] 'But we cannot', he writes, 'draw a hard-and-fast line, as some have sought to do, between what happens when there are unemployed resources and what happens when there is something more or less arbitrarily defined as full employment'.[35]

While it would be difficult to disagree with the latter sentence, one is left, I think, with the impression that Professor Robertson shows some reluctance to admit that most economists – including Keynes himself – who wrote about these matters before the publication of the *General Theory*, were guilty, at the opposite extreme, of neglecting the importance of changes in output. Of course, he is right to rebut the modern belief that the assumption of full employment was steadfastly maintained in the earlier works. It is only necessary to turn to the original text of *Money* to find some strongly-worded passages about the evils of unemployment, and the policies he advocates for the cure of depression scarcely imply constant real output! Moreover, apart from the prolonged discussion of the secular determinants of output in much of the pre-Keynesian literature, a great deal was said about the effect of short-period fluctuations on the demand for capital goods; after all, the Acceleration Principle has an ancient lineage. But it is a rather different matter when we turn to savings. That the volume of real income is one of the determinants of the volume of savings was clearly recognised, but the significance of this fact was not adequately appreciated: if there are unemployed resources, an increase in output stimulated by an increase in expenditure will raise the volume of savings.

It is difficult to feel entirely convinced by the treatment of these matters in the new introduction to *Banking Policy and the Price Level* in 1949, where Professor Robertson observes:

It is bound to remain to me a source of some bewilderment that at some time in the period following 1930, the idea that monetary analysis is concerned with the behaviour of output as a whole should apparently have struck Keynes, or at any rate, the able little group who were then advising him, with the force of a new discovery.

In the same paragraph he refers to a section in this book on the effect of hoarding, and explains that although the formal analysis was 'carried out on the simplify assumption that the production and sale of commodities remain unchanged . . . the ultimate concern of this section, as of the rest of the book (see the Table of Contents), was with changes in *output*'. This is all very difficult, and perhaps we, in turn, may express some bewilderment.

The changes in output discussed by Professor Robertson in his original texts were often structural, such as relative changes in the production of investment goods and consumption goods, or changes reflecting altered preferences as between income and leisure. The possibility of general deflation, or 'over-production', is considered in the *Study of Industrial Fluctuation*, but the treatment is somewhat equivocal. In his new Introduction to this book the author refers to his rough handling of Say's Law, but by modern standards it seems gentle enough; this is not surprising, for the Law is discussed before he has allowed for the effect of modern wage and money systems. Elsewhere there are stronger hints, such as his firm rebuttal of what came to be known as the Treasury View. There was a similar recognition of the effect of deflation on output in *Banking Policy and the Price Level*, and when he came to prepare the 1928 edition of *Money*, he included a chapter on policy which, if it were now to be published anonymously as a separate pamphlet, would undoubtedly be described as 'moderately Keynesian' by any reviewer who did not recognise it. Nevertheless, as he himself concedes, his main attention was devoted, even in 1928, to the problem of inflation, and he gives what is clearly the right explanation of an attitude which he shared with most other economists when he says:

> I had shaken down to what I was then justified in calling the 'common opinion' that, if this (i.e. inflation) could be avoided, there was good hope that the worst evils of trade depression could thereby be averted. In short, I shared the view that depression was a recurrent rather than an endemic malady.[36]

This view he now contrasts with 'the stagnation thesis'.

The theory of stagnation has been described as 'the essential content' of Keynes's theory in an article[37] by Professor John H. Williams, of which Professor Robertson has said 'I know of no shrewder appraisal of the "new economics . . . " '.[38] What is meant by 'the stagnation thesis'? Professor Williams answers this question by giving the following quotation from Keynes:

> The richer the community, the wider will tend to be the gap between its actual and its potential production; and therefore the more obvious

and outrageous the defects of the economic system. . . . Not only is the marginal propensity to consume weaker in a wealthy community, but, owing to its accumulation of capital being already larger, the opportunities for further investment are less attractive.

The prophecy that mature, wealthy, economies would suffer from stagnation has now been subjected to a great deal of criticism, and even Professor Hansen is no longer so robust a defender of the faith. This was Keynes at his most donnish and least scientific, and if the prophecy is 'the essential content' of his theory, then that theory may not, after all, be of major importance. But there is a more interesting line of thought running through these passages of the Keynesian literature, which we may call 'the theory of the weak boom'. It is a fact, not a prophecy, that some booms may be too weak to carry the economy to the point of 'full employment', and Keynes's theory was largely concerned with the implications of this fact. There was no need to suggest, as he did, that booms would continue to be weak and would, indeed, get weaker; for to take this further step was to make a dubious prophecy about developments in that long-run in which we are all dead. It was enough that, whatever the distant trend might be, the inter-war booms had been sufficiently weak (after 1920) to have made much of the earlier literature seem out of balance. If booms were weak, the analysis of inflation would be less interesting than the analysis of cyclical fluctuations in real income. If booms were weak, it would scarcely be plausible to hold that by moderating them, 'the worst evils of trade depression could thereby be averted'.[39] I believe it is here rather than in the theory of secular stagnation that 'the essential content' of Keynes's thought is to be found – or at all events part of that content.

Let us pose once again some of these questions about Professor Robertson's own ideas that are not clearly answered in his works. If he were describing afresh the principle features of the trade cycle, would he not place a good deal more emphasis on changes in the volume of output than he did before 1936 – although it is true that such changes were never ignored in his earlier work?[40] While continuing to stress the importance of changes in prices and in the distribution of income, topics which are somewhat neglected in the neo-Keynesian literature, would he not think it desirable to pay more attention than he formerly did to the effect on the volume of savings of variations in real national income – an effect which receives no more than a passing mention even in his remarkable essay of 1934?[41] If the answer to these questions should prove to be in the affirmative, it would seem to follow that the Keynesian contribution deserves a slightly more sympathetic treatment than it has received in his publications.

V

To borrow one of his own metaphors, Professor Robertson has always walked the tight-rope of policy with Blondinian skill. He could not, it is true, be called a Blondinian if there were substance in the belief that he is a firm opponent of 'compensatory fiscal measures' and an unrepentant believer in that old-fashioned nostrum, the rate of interest. But so simple a classification of so subtle an adviser reflects only confusion and misunderstanding. From his earliest writings he has adopted a many-sided approach, and his former belief that the excesses of the boom were the real cause of the depression did not prevent him from advocating vigorous action in order to stimulate a recovery.

In his first book (published in 1915) he rejected with scorn Mr Hawtrey's 'Treasury View' and gave his 'cordial' support to a policy of public investment as one of the remedies to be adopted in bad times. In the same book there is a plea for 'a saner and more centralised investment policy' (p. 266) and a proposal – to be accepted in substance about thirty years later in a great state document, the *White Paper on Employment Policy* – that 'a detailed report on new contracts for structural work or machinery should be compulsorily submitted to the Board of Trade'. Information about stocks should also, be held, be collected. Banking policy, briefly dealt with in this book, was naturally given a much fuller treatment in *Money*. In the 1928 edition[42] he was warning his readers that the rate of interest, while it would be of assistance and should certainly be employed, might not prove to be as efficacious as was sometimes hoped. Monetary policy was likely to be more powerful in checking a boom than in curing a depression, but even in the upswing it should be *qualitative* as well as *quantitative*. In the depression borrowing might still be insufficient because it might not be possible to reduce the rate of interest enough to entice sufficient borrowers – a proposition of central importance in the *General Theory*, where it was, however, supported by different arguments. In such circumstances there would be need for 'a more powerful ally – the Government of the country itself', armed with a policy of counter-cyclical expenditure. Moreover, interest policy might sometimes conflict with communal needs which were imperfectly represented on the market:

> The present generation seems to have made up its mind about the provision of working class houses; and he must be a bold man who, knowing and visualising all the relevant social facts, declares that it is wrong. Now once such a decision has been deliberately taken it seems merely vexatious to hamper its execution by forcing the enterprise in question to submit to the ordeal by rate of interest. In such circumstances it may fairly be urged that the banks, being, when all is said and done, the servants of the community, should be instructed or exhorted or entreated to give effect to its wishes by putting a generous ration of loans at the disposal of the neglected enterprise.[43]

Professor Robertson would have earned applause in rather different quarters if, twenty years later, he had merely repeated passages such as these from his earlier writings instead of delivering a new lecture on 'The Economic Outlook'.[44]

Enough has been said, I hope, to indicate the wide range of Robertsonian policy and to give some impression of the modernity of what he said so many years ago. Yet it was, I suspect, the very enlightenment of his own views which made it difficult for Professor Robertson to appreciate the revolution in thought which followed the publication of the *General Theory*. *Twenty years* before Keynes published his *magnum opus*, Professor Robertson had attacked the fallacy behind the Treasury View, but the validity of his criticism had not been generally accepted. His arguments were further developed and set out at greater length in the twenties, and he was supported by some of his colleagues – notably Keynes himself. Progress was made, but the fact remains that remnants of the Treasury View persisted. A great change in outlook was required, and Keynes, heavily engaged as he always was in the thick of the fight, formed a clear notion of the strength of the opposition. In the end it was his rhetoric and his new mystique which carried the day, although Professor Robertson's earlier attacks contributed in no small measure to his success.

VI

However easy it may be to show that Keynesian ideas were less original than some of their exponents have been wont to suggest, the effect of the 'New Economics', viewed as a whole, was immensely impressive, and the change in emphasis which followed its acceptance was appropriate enough in the circumstances of the time. But circumstances alter with disconcerting speed, and since the outbreak of the war part of the 'new economics' has been irrelevant, although it is only fair to add that the study of the national income, which derived so powerful a stimulus from Keynes's conceptual framework, is as valuable in times of inflation as in times of deflation. On the face of it, it might have been expected that the older theories of instability, which were so much concerned with in-flation, would then have come back into favour, but these theories needed to be substantially modified in order to allow for the effect of controls and in order to relate the reasoning more closely to the national income concepts. For example, the assumption that real wages would fall while profits and, with them, corporate and personal savings, were inflated, does not seem to be altogether in harmony with recent ex-perience. If the Keyesian 'economics of depression' has not been ap-plicable, neither has the economics of open inflation; a third category, the economics of suppressed inflation, has had to be evolved. No doubt Keynes himself, who was always so exhilarated by these swift changes in circumstances, would have continued to work on this new task which he had already begun in his pamphlet, *How to Pay for the War*; his followers, for their part, have not been the most backward in doing so.

It must, nevertheless, be conceded that some ideas, which had their origin in the *General Theory* or were greatly strengthened by it, have had an unfavourable effect on what may call 'middle-brow-opinion'. Of these, the first we need mention is the belief that the main threat to the level of employment is always too little monetary expenditure. Thus it is sometimes held that, if we cannot hope to hit exactly the right level of expenditure, it is wise to err a little on the side of inflation rather than risk some unemployment. To argue thus is to overlook the fact that too much monetary expenditure may create mass unemployment if it brings disaster to the balance of payments of a country which is heavily dependent upon imported raw materials; an inflationary full-employment policy may therefore defeat its own object. This is one of the lessons which Professor Robertson, for his part, has sought to teach.[45]

A second consequence of the 'New Economics' has been a too exclusive emphasis on budgetary policy as a means of controlling monetary expenditure. Enough has been said to show that Professor Robertson was one of the first to express scepticism about what could be done by means of the rate of interest and to advocate what is now called 'functional finance'; but the reaction against banking policy, when it came, went too far, and Professor Robertson, preoccupied as usual with the disheartening task of trying to advance a balanced view, has given many unpopular warnings about the danger of placing 'too big a burden on the broad shoulders of Police-Constable Public Finance'. He has reminded us that 'Sir Stafford Crippses . . . do not grow on every gooseberry bush', and even when there is a Crippsian determination, severe damage may be done if taxation is raised to a very high level. As usually happens, the events have run ahead of popular theory. Banking policy was dethroned and exiled, and budgetary policy exalted in its stead; but while this was going on, the burden of state expenditure was sapping the victor's strength. If the budget is to be the principal method of checking inflation, the sums needed to meet public expenditure must not stretch the somewhat inelastic limits of taxable capacity too tightly; otherwise it becomes necessary to choose between an inadequate surplus on the one hand and, on the other, a level of taxation that cannot be reconciled with the needs of healthy industrial development. Functional finance had not been rendered impotent, but it has been sufficiently weakened by heavy public spending to justify the restoration, as an additional and reinforcing measure, of the old-fashioned policy of credit control. Professor Robertson's advice was taken at last in 1951 and 1952 – and if it is held that this was rather late in the day to do so because the inflationary gap had become less menacing, it may be replied, first, that the gap had by no means disappeared, and, secondly, that, as Professor Robertson has pointed out, there is a close connection between credit policy and wage inflation.[46]

It takes a great deal of optimism to suppose that no harm will be done, even in a period of strong inflationary pressure, by providing an elastic supply of credit on easy terms. I find it difficult to believe that Keynes would have held so sanguine a view and the following observation by Professor John H. Willaims is of no small interest: 'Keynes changed his mind, and almost the last time I saw him was complaining that the easy money policy had been greatly overdone, and interest rates were too low both in England and here'.[47] The fact remains that the creed of cheap money – the faith that defies economic vicissitude – grew out of Keynes's 'economics of depression'.

The last feature of the neo-Keynesian recommendations with which we shall deal is the proposal that investment should be stabilised. Doubts have been expressed about the extent to which such a policy can be implemented so long as large sectors of industry remain in private hands, and the controversy has, I think, mainly centred around this question of enforcement. But is it really true that a stable volume of investment is a wise objective? Or rather, since it is bound to be a question of degree, how much stability do we want and what price are we prepared to pay for it? Over a period of many years. Professor Robertson has been asking these questions, and I suspect that the sooner we face the fundamental issues he has raised, the less likely are we to be disillusioned by the outcome of full-employment policies. Professor Robertson, it need scarcely be said, has always recognised that there are secondary, or induced, declines in investment during a downswing, and the case for preventing 'a purposeless and obscene orgy of destruction'[48] is not in doubt. But periodic variations in the utility of investment goods must be expected, and these variations can be ignored only at the expense of sacrifices in other directions which may become excessive. 'To a large extent, in the writer's view, fluctuations in the desirability of acquiring instruments are the inevitable penalty of industrial progress'.[49] Since the war, investment, though restricted, has probably been at a higher level than a policy of cyclical stabilisation would have warranted, but it is not surprising that we should have allowed more immediate needs to govern our decisions about the number of houses, factories, ships and machines we should try to construct. Some fluctuations in investment are desirable and some are not. Professor Robertson's work on the trade cycle has been largely concerned with distinguishing between the two in the hope that means can be found 'to limit the turbulence, without destroying the vitality' of industrial change.

VII

We have now worked backwards from the study of policy to Professor Robertson's views on the trade cycle. No attempt can be made here to assess his immense contribution, but it may at least be possible to indicate his method of approach. Professor Robertson, whose views are similar in some ways to Schumpeter's, has laid great, though not exclusive, emphasis on innovations as a cause of the cycle. He has tended to regard the cycle as an aspect of industrial progress, and to infer that the nature of the fluctuations cannot be understood if the study of them is isolated from the study of industry. By contrast, most of what has been written on the trade cycle in this country at least, has been concerned with the construction of models which will display a self-persistent cycle. Instead of trying to discover and to analyse the main 'strategic factors' that may govern the course of the cycle,[50] the authors of these models have reduced the number of factors to the minimum consistent with perpetual motion. There has been, of course, a partial justification for this method, and much has been learned from the 'endogenous' models so constructed. But there has been some tendency to forget – what no one would explicitly deny – that these models are only preliminary exercises from which many factors have been excluded either because they are 'unnecessary' or because they cannot easily be given a mathematical form. Thus the cyclical changes in the distribution of income, to which Professor Robertson has given so much attention, now tend to be ignored; and, to an even greater degree, the complex process of industrial change has suffered from more or less chronic neglect. Without questioning the usefulness of the work done by the model-makers, I would suggest that their methods have received too exclusive attention, and to this I would add that there has been a parallel tendency to place a too exclusive reliance upon the methods of those 'latter-day wizards, the econometricians'. But I cannot do better than quote Professor Robertson's own remarks about the various ways in which the trade cycle has been studied:

> As to stylised models of the cycle, of the kind now so fashionable, they doubtless have their uses, provided their limitations are clearly understood. We must wait with respectful patience while the econometricians decide whether their elaborate methods are really capable of covering such models with flesh and blood. But I confess that to me at least the forces at work seem so complex, the question whether even the few selected parameters can be relied on to stay put through the cycle or between cycles so doubtful, that I wonder whether more truth will not in the end be wrung from interpretative studies of the crude data of the general type contained in this volume, but more intensive, more scrupulously worded and more expert.[51]

VIII

We have already noted the main points of conflict between Robertson and Keynes, some of them attributable to verbal difficulties, others real enough; in conclusion it may be illuminating to attempt the regrettably unfamiliar exercise of recording how much they have in common. We are not sure how much Professor Robertson would now modify his earlier analysis; this difficulty will continue to perplex us, but I believe it is possible to argue that the points on which he and Keynes are in agreement are more important than those on which they differ. In attempting to support this claims, I shall confine most of my attention to Keynes's own works and neglect in the main those of his followers – a vaguely defined group, in which many conflicting views are represented. I shall use terms derived from various sources, not, I hope, inconsistently, but with little tenderness for that strange academic prudery which seems to afflict some of Keynes's supporters.

The controversy about savings and investment need not detain us. The terms are used in two different senses in the *General Theory*; Keynes failed to distinguish between these senses, and the stubbornness with which he and some of his followers defended his position was responsible for much needless dispute; but the error can be corrected without upsetting Keynes's argument, and it is probably true that outside Cambridge this particular controversy is now dead. We may therefore say that both Keynes and Robertson are in agreement on the central proposition that the amount people try to save may diverge from the amount people try to invest, with consequent changes in total monetary outlay. If this proposition, taken by itself and without reference to their controversy, now sounds almost too obvious to be worth advancing, it is well to remember that its general acceptance, at least in this country, was largely achieved by the combined efforts of Robertson and Keynes. Savings and investment may diverge because the rate of interest does not act as the equilibrating factor it was once supposed to be.[52] To say this is not to deny that savings and investment can have some direct effect on the rate of interest. Here Keynes tended to advocate a view that was unnecessary for his main thesis. It would have been enough to say that there are other forces at work of sufficient importance to promote a major fluctuation in monetary outlay, and Professor Robertson, for his part, has long since emphasised that this is in fact what happens. In this connection the contribution of the *General Theory* was twofold: it emphasised the importance of changes in the desire to hold idle balances, and it drew attention to the need for further study of the motives that lead people to want such balances. There is still a good deal of uncertainty about the manner in which hoarders behave, and the links between different parts of the capital market, different rates of interest and different security prices are by no means clear. To pretend that there is a settled body of opinion about these matters would be absurd, but that is not the immediate point at issue. What we are concerned with is to say that although there has been a mountain of misunderstanding, for which Keynes must bear much of the blame, there appears to be no irreconcilable conflict between his basic ideas and those of Professor Robertson.

One of the principal changes brought about by the Keynesian Revolution was to lay greater stress on the effect of changes in real income. Here we can only ask whether Professor Robertson would not agree that this was desirable in the circumstances of the time, even if, as so often happens, the change of emphasis went too far. Would he himself not now be inclined to pay rather more attention than he did in some of his earlier works to the occurrence of weak booms?[53] Here too, Keynes went too far, momentarily intrigued as he was by his prophecy of stagnation; but it is not hard to trace a path of compromise, provided some realistic allowance is made for the differences between cycles. The propensity to consume was over-simplified by Keynes, and the theory of the multiplier unduly exalted. But would Professor Robertson, for his part, be prepared to concede that the size of the marginal propensity to consume, whether steady or not, is a critical factor – not merely 'a potentially useful little brick and one which his own earlier models neglected?'

In reviewing Professor Robertson's recommendations for the control of the trade cycle, I have already commented on their Keynesian flavour. Perhaps I should have said that Keynes's recommendations have a Robertsonian flavour, but my concern is not with historical precedence, an almost insoluble issue in any case, but with the marked degree of similarity between their views. This similarity appears more striking when it is recalled that Keynes's own views, as expounded, for example, in *The Times* in 1936, were a good deal more modest than some of those now entertained about 'full employment'. In matters of policy I suspect that the main difference was one of general outlook. Keynes always tended to be optimistic about what could be done; his recommendations were advanced with confidence, and he seems to have felt that great improvements could be made if people with the right ideas were in charge of affairs. By contrast the author of 'On Sticking to One's Last'[54] has always appeared cautious, more impressed by the uncertainty of the future and more dubious about the infallibility of even the best of advisers. Keynes's belief in what could be done with clever men in control, and his impatience with those who obstructed their path formed a certain bond of sympathy between him and the supporters of rigorous economic planning, but his temperamental bias did not lead him to abandon his belief in a liberal economy before the war. We need not embark upon much dubious speculation about the extent to which Keynes would have favoured the use of controls in post-war Britain; some may suspect that before his death he had begun to believe in such planning to a much greater extent than Professor Robertson but the evidence is conflicting; at all events his work on international trade scarcely implied that he had lost faith in the price mechanism. Moreover, his famous letter to Professor Hayek, though it revealed a divergence of views, showed that he was not prepared to dismiss as absurd the fear that we might drift unwittingly down the road to serfdom.[55] The trade cycle receives only scanty treatment in the *General Theory* and in Keynes's subsequent writings, but there is sufficient evidence to suggest that his general approach was not altogether dissimilar to Professor Robertson's. Admittedly the theory of the multiplier seems to imply a belief in at least one key parameter, but to my mind the general tone of the book, with its heavy emphasis on volatile expectations, is hostile to the view that elaborate mechanical models can provide a sufficiently realistic explanation of the trade cycle. Moreover, the classical attack on econometrics was delivered by Keynes himself in his review of Professor Tinbergen's work, and his criticism was strong and forthright as compared with the misgivings gently expressed from time to time by Professor Robertson. It was unfortunate that Keynes was unable to develop his ideas on the cycle, and it is still more unfortunate that Professor Robertson, for his part, has not taken the opportunity to revise those theories which originally made such an impressive contribution to the subject. The *Study of Industrial Fluctuation*, great book though it is, is out of date, as its author would be the first to admit; in particular, the subtle analysis of industrial change that it contains needs to be related to a more modern theory of effective demand. In the books and articles that appeared between the *Study* and the appearance of the *General Theory*, Professor Robertson did in fact go a long way towards making this relationship plain; but a good deal has happened since then, and it has surely not all been in vain. Presumably there are some points in the Keynesian theory which should now be incorporated in the Robertsonian account of the cycle. The neo-Keynesians, for their part, have been primarily interested in mechanistic constructions in which great aggregates move along predestined courses; the complexity of industrial growth, the structural changes that accompany the cycle, the connection between economic progress and the instability of investment – these and many related topics have tended to go out of fashion. Admittedly we have learned a great deal from the study of mechanical models, and it would, I think, be a great mistake to imply that we must choose between the two methods of approach; both are needed. We have also learned a great deal from the controversies about savings, investment and liquidity preference that have occupied so much of Professor Robertson's attention in recent years. But one cannot altogether suppress the suspicion that the most important task has been largely neglected – that of combining some of Keynes's innovations with Professor Robertson's own theory of industrial instability. Such a combination would surely provide us with a more impressive and realistic account of cyclical fluctuations than has yet been evolved.

NOTES

1.   D. H. Robertson, *Banking Policy and the Price Level* (New York: Augustus M. Kelly, 1949). Unfortunately there has been no new English edition of this scarce and important work.

2.   W. Fellner, 'The Robertsonian Evolution', *American Economic Review*, June 1952. See pp. 127–47 below.

3.   J. R. Hicks, 'The Monetary Theory of D. H. Robertson', *Economica*, February 1942.

4.   R. Harrod, *Life of John Maynard Keynes* (London: Macmillan, 1951) p. 451.

5.   J. R. Hicks, *Value and Capital*, pp. 153 et seq. Robertson himself has said as much. C.f. DHR *Essays in Monetary Theory* (London: P. S. King and Son, 1940) pp. 9–10; DHR *Utility and All That* (London: Allen & Unwin 1953 p. 105).

6.   My views have been developed more fully in the *Fluctuations in Income and Employment* (London: Pitman, 1946 3rd ed., Ch. 11, and in 'A Reconsideration of the Theory of Effective Demand', *Economica*, 1947.

7.   C.f. e.g., the list of possible constituents on p. 3 of D. H. Robertson, *Essays in Monetary Theory*, *op. cit.*

8.   Ibid., p. 24. But the transition from short run to long needs more extended treatment than it receives here. Nor do I feel that this matter has been completely cleared up even in the essay. 'Some Notes on the Theory of Interest', *Utility and All That*, *op. cit.*, Ch. 6.

9.   In this connection it is interesting to recall Keynes's attempt to degrade the Quantity Equations from the rank of truisms to the rank of untruths (DHR, 'Mr Keynes's Theory of Money', *Economic Journal*, 1931, p. 396). This is, to my mind, one of the most puzzling features of his work, and it is disconcerting to find that Mr Harrod, in discussing Professor Robertson's review of Keynes's *Treatise of Money*, (Macmillan, 1930) seems to support the conclusion that his reviewers had simply failed to grasp what it was he was denying. While he fully recognized and dis-

cussed at length the causal relations, both simple and complex, between the divergence of investment from saving on the one hand, and changes in the quantity of money and velocity of its circulation on the other, he had emphatically denied that an inflationary or deflationary movement was normally caused or *necessarily accompanied* by the latter kind of changes (ibid., p. 435 (my italics)). In this Keynes was surely in error.

10. J. M. Keynes, *General Theory* (London: Macmillan, 1936) p. 174.

11. H. Willard, 'Monetary Theory', Ch. 9, in *A Survey of Contemporary Economics*, edited by Howard S. Ellis (Philadelphia: Blakiston, 1948). C.f. Robertson, *Essays in Monetary Theory*, op. cit., p. 17: There are inevitable difficulties in expressing in statically-framed terms the situation existing at *a moment of time during a period of change.* . . .

12. It may be helpful at this point to look at two examples in both of which the total amount of money is assumed to be constant. (i) Suppose liquidity preference grows stronger. More money is now demanded for L_2 purposes, but more is not available because M is constant and M_1 is assumed to be a function of Y. The rate must then rise till speculators are content to hold the existing stock of securities. There will, of course, be further repercussions that will affect Y, M_1 and M_2, but the initial change in the rate of interest has come about without any change in M_2. (ii) Suppose there is a change in the demand for investable funds or a change in savings – the more relevant case if we are considering the proposition that productivity and thrift cannot affect the rate of interest. If, for example, new securities are floated, the rate of interest will tend to fall, but this tendency must be offset if the rate is to be determined, as Keynes holds it is, by liquidity preference and the amount of money. It is here that a change in M_2 balances is indispensable to the Keynesian theory. For the rate can only be prevented from rising if speculators buy more securities and run down their M_2 balances accordingly that is say, if they dishoard. The change in balances is not associated with a change in the rate of interest; it is rather the factor that prevents such a change and thus allows total monetary expenditure to alter. (C.f. J. M. Keynes, *op. cit.*, p. 201 et seg.). These two cases are sometimes confused, and the role of hoarding and dishoarding consequently misunderstood. (Both examples are, of course, highly simplified.)

13. DHR, *Money* (Cambridge: Cambridge University Press, 1st ed. 1922; 1948) p. 213.

14. Keynes held that the ratio between Y and M_1 +M_2 was without significance. This seems an unduly harsh judgement. What then is to be said about the various definitions in the Keynesian theory? Is the ex post equality between S and I without significance? C.f. J. M. Keynes, *op. cit.*, p. 209 n.4.

15. Robertson, *Utility and All That* (London: George Allen & Unwin, 1952) p. 107.

16.   DHR, *Essays in Monetary Theory*, pp. 24–5n. The quotation from the Minutes of Evidence of the Committee is as follows: '(*Witness*). What it comes to is this, that a large part of what appears to be the rate of interest on long-dated securities is now really a premium for risk, or believed risk, and the long rate of interest remains high compared with Bank rate because it contains a large element of what are really profits, the reward for real or imaginary risks.' (Macmillan Committee on Finance and Industry, April 1930.)

17.   C.f. Robertson, *Essays in Monetary Theory*, p. 21.

18.   The expression is Mr Harrod's, *op. cit.*, p. 456.

19.   C.f. Keynes, 'Alternative Theories of the Rate of Interest', *Economic Journal*, June 1937, p. 249. The novelty in my treatment of saving and investment consists, not in my maintaining their necessary equality, but in the proposition that it is not the rate of interest, but the level of income which (in conjunction with certain other factors) ensures their equality.

20.   DHR, *Money*, p. 209.

21.   H. Johnson, 'Some Cambridge Controversies in Monetary Theory', *Review of Economic Studies*, 1951–2, No. 49, pp. 93–4.

22.   Even in the short-period, such complications can be important: the proportion of income consumed fell during the cyclical recovery in the United States between 1921 and 1923, but the fall did not continue between 1923 and 1929, which were years of fairly steady progress when real income per head rose substantially. C.f. T Wilson, *op. cit.*, XIII; F. Modigliani, Fluctuations in the Saving-Income Ratio, *Studies in Income and Wealth*, vol. II.

23.   T. Duesenberry, *Income, Saving, and the Theory of Consumer Behaviour* (Cambridge, Mass.: Harvard University Press, 1949).

24.   L. Metzler, 'Three Lags in the Circular Flow of Income', in *Income, Employment and Public Policy, Essays in Honour of Alvin H. Hansen* (New York: W. W. Norton, 1948) Ch. 1.

25.   It may be noted that Professor J. R. Hicks has used both Robertsonian lags to good effect in his exposition of the Mutliplier in *A Contribution to the Theory of the Trade Cycle* (Oxford: Clarendon Press, 1950).

26.   DHR, *Money*, p. 207.

27.   W. Beveridge, *Full Employment in a Free Society* (London: Allen & Unwin, 1944) pp. 337–8.

28.   After all, one of the leading Keynesians – Mr R. F. Harrod – has argued more strongly than anyone else that investment has been excessive since the war.

29.   DHR, 'Effective Demand and the Multiplier', in *Essays in Monetary Theory*, *op. cit.*, Ch. ix.

30.   DHR, *Money*, p. 211–12.

31.   A. Marshall, *Principles of Economics* (London: Macmillan, 1880) pp. 710–11.

32. DHR, Effective Demand and the Multiplier', *Essays in Monetary Theory*, *op. cit.*, p. 120.

33. DHR, 'Effective Demand and the Multiplier', *op. cit.*

34. DHR, *Money*, *op. cit.*, p. 204. The reference is to Mrs J. Robinson's article 'The Theory of Money and Analysis of Output', in the *Review of Economic Studies*, 1933–4, p. 26. Her remark is a little ambiguous. It may be objected that one of the principal features of Keynesian thought was its insistence on the link between monetary expenditure and output; the suggestion that the two be divorced may therefore seem a little strange. But this is not, I suspect, what she had in mind, and her meaning could probably be conveyed more clearly by deleting a theory of money in the quotation above and substituting a theory of the value of money. This is clearly how Robertson has interpreted the passage.

35. DHR, *Money*, pp. 204–5. It may be recalled that Mrs Robinson herself stressed this very point in Chapter 1 of *Essays in the Theory of Employment* (Oxford: Blackwell, 1937).

36. DHR, *Money*, p. 214.

37. John H. Williams, 'An Appraisal of Keynesian Economics', *Proceedings of the American Economic Association*, 38, May 1948.

38. DHR, 'Some Notes on the Theory of Interest', Loc. cit. p. 97.

39. DHR, *Money*, p. 214.

40. C.f. the new 'Introduction' to *A Study of Industrial Fluctuation* (London: London School of Economics, 1948) p. ix.

41. DHR, 'Industrial Fluctuation and the Natural Rate of Interest', Ch. V in *Essays in Monetary Theory*, pp. 85–6.

42. In particular, DHR, *Money* (1928 ed.) Ch. VIII.

43. DHR, *Money*, p. 173.

44. The lecture was delivered to Section F of the British Association and presented as 'The Economic Outlook', *Economic Journal*, December 1947, pp. 421–37.

45. DHR, 'What Has Happened to the Rate of Interest?' in *Utility and All That*, Ch. 5, p. 92.

46. DHR, 'What Happened to the Rate of Interest?' Loc. cit., p. 90–2.

47. J. H. Williams, 'An Economist's Confessions', *American Economic Review*, March 1952, p. 14. But some of Keynes's followers do not appear to have accepted this view, C.f. Harrod's defence of cheap money even in 1947: *Are These Hardships Necessary?* pp. 124, et. seq.

48. DHR, The Snake and the Worm, *Essays in Monetary Theory*, p. 105.

49. DHR, *Banking Policy and the Price Level*, p. 94.

50. C.f. J. H. Williams, 'An Economist's Confessions', *American Economic Review*, vol. 42, March 1952.

51. DHR, *A Study of Industrial Fluctuation*, pp. xvi–xvii.

52. One has to be careful at this point. Many of the earlier economists recognised that the rate of interest might not be allowed to do its job

during an expansion, but they were reluctant to admit as much about a contraction. I have already referred to this asymmetry in classical thought in the first chapter of T. Wilson, *Fluctuations in Income and Employment, op. cit.*

53.   Weak booms are in fact discussed in his two famous essays, 'The Snake and the Worm' and 'The Trade Cycle – An Academic View', both reprinted in DHR, *Essays in Monetary Theory, op. cit.*

54.   DHR, 'On Sticking to One's Last', *Economic Journal*, December 1949.

55.   R. Harrod, loc. cit., p. 436–7. The letter also reveals his optimism about what can be done with the right people in control. Moderate planning will be safe if those carrying it out are rightly orientated in their own minds and hearts to the moral issue. This is in fact already true of some of them. But the curse is that there is also an important section who could almost be said to want planning not in order to enjoy its fruits but because morally they hold ideas exactly the opposite to yours, and wish to serve not God but the devil. He appears confident that this evil could be exorcised, though the grounds for his confidence remain obscure.

7 The Robertsonian Evolution

William Fellner

THE TRIAD

Dennis Holme Robertson first published *A Study of Industrial Fluctuation* in 1915, *Money* in 1922, and *Banking Policy and the Price Level* in 1926.[1] In the early post-war period these volumes were reprinted,[2] all three with new introductions and *Money* also with two new chapters. To the *Study* the London School appended an article by Marcel Labordère, with an introduction by Professor Robertson.[3]

The sequence in which these works were first published expresses a gradual broadening of Robertson's approach. In the *Study* we find detailed historical discussion and theoretical analysis of basic dynamic forces such as inventions, the durability and indivisibility of real capital, gestation periods, good and bad harvests, but we find comparatively little monetary analysis; *Money* contains a classic treatment of the essential influence (non-neutrality) of monetary phenomena; and *Banking Policy* is unmistakably rooted in the two previous works. A reader knows more about Robertson's views on money and employment if he has studied *Banking Policy* and, in addition, some of the author's later contributions, perhaps mainly those reprinted in his *Essays in Monetary Theory*,[4] than if he substitutes one of the earlier volumes for *Banking Policy*. But acquaintance with the earlier volumes makes it much easier to comprehend the highly concise treatment in the hundred pages of which *Banking Policy* consists. In the present article the reader will find merely a sketchy summary, most of it on pp. 130–3.

Over sixty years have elapsed since the original publication of the last of these three books. There are many ways in which works of the nineteen-twenties can still be 'interesting' to the 'interested' reader. Much has happened in the world since that time, and much has happened in economics. The economics of money and the level of employment (level of business activity) with which we will be here mainly concerned has gone through its Keynesian and post-Keynesian period, and the product which emerged after many years of heated controversy is different is essential respects from that which existed before. What makes a specific contribution of the preceding era significant enough to justify the contemporary theorist's interest in studying it in the original? Has it not all been absorbed by more recent currents? Is it not 'merely' the historian of doctrine in us who turns to these books? After all, what educated person is completely disinterested in the antecedents of the work in which he tries to participate? Is this all?

This in itself would not be as little as it can be made to sound. But it is *not* all. After so many years, a surprisingly small part of Robertson's early contribution is outmoded in the sense that a problem with which it is concerned seems to have lost its significance, or in the sense that a statement is clearly less adequate than later statements of other authors on the same subject. More frequently will the reader encounter analysis which will strike him as a point of departure toward those constituents of the subsequent New Economics which presumably have come to stay. In a good many instances he will wonder what other paths, besides those which were opened up in the nineteen-thirties and the nineteen-forties, could be made to originate in Robertsonian analysis. Such speculations are essentially forward-looking. They should prove more fruitful than attempts to rank and grade the great contributions of recent decades.

ROBERTSON AND THE NEW ECONOMICS

Shortly after the first impact of Keynes's *General Theory* was felt, Keynesianism started acquiring at least two different meanings. There were those who saw the essence of the doctrine in the theory of stagnation. There were others who believed that the fundamental Keynesian contribution was to develop a new apparatus which focuses attention on the inability of the market mechanism continuously to equate voluntary savings to investment at a satisfactory level of employment. In the second of these two interpretations the words 'to develop a new apparatus' deserve all the emphasis that can be placed on them. The apparatus did indeed have many novel features. The notion that the market mech-

anism fails automatically to resolve the problem of effective demand
was of course not new. Nor was the interest in compensatory central-
bank and government policies, including public works programmes.

To some of the best minds of the preceding decades the problem of
effective demand had posed itself as a problem of outstanding significance; and, especially from the second half of the nineteen-twenties
on, most then 'modern' economists came to believe that fruitful analysis of effective demand requires connecting the problem with the
relationship between saving and investing. The Keynes of the late nineteen-twenties – that is to say, Keynes up to about his fiftieth year, and
particularly in the fifth decade of his life – should be classed among a
group of economists who were developing the savings-investment framework with the intention of making it increasingly applicable to effec-
tive-demand analysis. The Keynes of the late nineteen-twenties did
this with great brilliance and originality but he did it in a tradition which
by then had become well established. The tradition was of mixed origin,
certainly of Swedish as well as of British, even though the Swedish
(Wicksellian) influence came down to him very indirectly. Keynes's
Treatise on Money, his first major contribution to this kind of theory,
was published in 1930, four years after Robertson's *Banking Policy
and the Price Level*.

In the *General Theory* Keynes made his readers feel that he had
broken away from the established tradition. He truly did, if it was his
intention to provide a point of departure for the doctrine of chronic
stagnation. He did not if he meant to develop a theory which was useful
for a general analysis of discrepancies between full-employment equilibrium and deficient-or-excessive effective demand. Even in this case
he contributed a great deal that is of lasting significance. But in this
case there was no Keynesian Revolution. There merely was evolutionary progress along Wicksellian-Robertsonian-Keynesian lines; and the
heritage of the next generation will be just as essentially Robertsonian
and Swedish as Keynesian, regardless of what they will choose to call it.

The present writer feels uncertain as to whether this interpretation of
Keynes is more or less adequate than the stagnationist (more genuinely
'revolutionary') interpretation. It is probable that the truth is somewhere
in the middle. Keynes, I think, must have intended to make additions to
the house in general, not merely to enlarge and furnish its stagnationist

corner and to tear down the rest. But he was particularly interested in the stagnationist corner and he tried to make it stand out more prominently than the other parts of the house. At any rate, regardless of what his intentions were, this is what he actually accomplished. Furthermore, the great influence of the *General Theory* is largely a consequence of the fact that it is easy to 'correct' the Keynesian structure in such a way as to reduce the prominence of the stagnationist corner. I do not mean to imply that at present the long-run validity of the stagnation thesis can be disproved or proved. Nor is it clear at all that stagnant tendencies, if they should become predominant under mature capitalism, will properly be interpreted along Keynesian lines rather than along those developed by Schumpeter in his *Capitalism, Socialism and Democracy*. It is merely suggested here that in the present era of economic history few persons would be interested in a theory which is unequivocally built around the central theme of deflationary tendencies and of stagnation. In fact, many are interested in the Keynesian theory and rightly so. This is because something does remain of it even after the stagnationist corner has been reduced to proper dimensions.

The remainder is, of course, not *identical* with the Robertsonian structure. The specifically Keynesian contribution stays significant in whatever way we look at it. On the other hand, Keynesian economics left unexploited much that was significant in the Robertsonian and other pre-Keynesian contributions. Evolutionary progress then requires adding parts of the Keynesian achievement onto the structure which by the end of the nineteen-twenties had reached height; and it requires also an interest in developing the neglected elements of the pre-Keynesian monetary economics. The structure, in its pre-Keynesian stage, was by no means exclusively of Robertson's making. But Robertson played a significant role in erecting it.

ROBERTSONIAN ECONOMICS AND THE BASIC ELEMENTS
OF THE KEYNESIAN APPARATUS

Robertsonian theory is dynamic in that it depicts a *process* of economic development. Furthermore, it does not assume that this process satisfies the conditions of moving equilibrium. In contrast, the formal apparatus of the *General Theory* treats the determinants of aggregate output and employment for a single time-interval during which the system reaches a state of equilibrium, with the result that if the economic process (which is not described by the formal apparatus) consisted of continuous movements from one such condition to the next, then the observed path could be considered one of moving (or dynamic) equilibrium. To be sure, verbally or informally, Keynes did express significant views about the process itself, and also about what the shape of the equilibrium-determining functions is likely to be during the time-intervals which he expected to become typical under mature capitalism. If we emphasize this 'informal' part of the story, then we direct our attention to the forecast that we are moving toward a chronic insufficiency of effective demand, presumably with qualifications relating to hot and to cold wars and the like. The apparatus itself is more general. It shows that effective demand *may* be too small to make the equilibrium conditions compatible with full employment; or that it *may* be just sufficient for accomplishing this; or that it *may* be too great for accomplishing it at stable prices. The Keynesian apparatus establishes this result by looking at the economy during a time interval through which it passes in the course of a process. Post-Keynesian economists who wished to place the apparatus back into the context of a process had to reintroduce links between periods, in the Robertsonian or in some alternative fashion (e.g. in the Neo-Wicksellian). Here moving equilibrium becomes merely a special case.

In the Robertsonian schema, savings are defined as the difference between the income earned in the recent past – i.e., in the preceding short period – and the consumption expenditure of the present period. Hence, movements in money income can be expressed in terms of the relationship between investment (I) and savings (S). I>S means rising money income, S>I means falling money income, and S=I means that money income remains unchanged. Such a schema implies a relationship in the nature of the 'consumption function', since consumption expenditure is related to disposable income (which here is defined as income previously earned) but the Robertsonian analysis allows for further causal factors which influence the saving-ratio out of disposable income. The size of cash balances, the rate of interest, and relative prices belong among these factors, although they do not exhaust the list.

In the Robertsonian system the relationship of investment to saving may be said to determine the movements in money income, but it is possible to explain these movements alternatively in terms of quantity equations. These may be either of the transactions or the cash balance type. An excess of investment over saving, that is, a rise in money income, must for example be accompanied by a rise in the stock of money and/or a rise in its income velocity, i. e., either by a rise in the money stock or by a fall in liquidity ratios which are reciprocals of velocities. At any rate, once we are faced with a change (say, with a rise) in money income, the quantity theory framework provides a convenient point of departure for a discussion of the question of how much of this change will show as a change in real output and how much as a change in prices. Such a discussion leads ultimately into the problem of supply elasticities. These, in addition to the monetary savings-investment relations, must be known for translating the movements of monetary aggregates into movements in real output and employment.

While saving takes place 'out of' disposable income, trends in investment are explained mainly by technological and organisational progress and other structural changes which influence the composition of output as well is its aggregate size. The long-run inducement to invest is interpreted as emanating from specific sectors of the economy and emphasis is placed on the fact that changes in the structure of costs and demands affect the size of aggregate demand and output. Technological improvement is presumably the most significant, but not the only secular (log-run) factor which, by way of its direct effect on specific industries, gives rise to changes in aggregate output. In a more detailed discussion of the investment process it is then stressed that indivisibilities, the acceleration-principle mechanism, and the existence of gestation periods (production-lags) complicate the outcome considerably. In other words, 'cyclical' considerations are worked into the investment discussion which is largely rooted in the analysis of long-run factors.

So far we have encountered in the Robertsonian system two determinants of aggregate output which may be said to 'correspond' to Keynesian determinants, namely, the income-consumption relationship, and the rate of return on investment (marginal efficiency). In addition, attention has been called to several Robertsonian elements of reasoning which do not have a Keynesian equivalent (such as the quantity-theory link between changes in money flows and changes in prices and output respectively; the effect of changes in the composition of aggregates on their total size; the period-sequence analysis, etc.). To these distinctive elements I shall return later. At present let us see how far we can go in drawing parallels. So far we have been concerned with the Robertsonian version of the 'consumption function' and of the 'marginal efficiency of capital'. However, in Robertson as in Keynes, the amount of new investment depends on interest-rates as well as on the marginal efficiency. What about the rate of interest?

The Robertsonian treatment of the determinants of the interest-rate runs in terms of the loanable funds approach. The relationship between this approach and the Keynesian liquidity-preference theory has received much attention in the literature. I think it may now be stated that the two, when viewed as general approaches or frameworks, do not differ essentially, if allowance is made for 'finance' in the liquidity theory. In this event the differences are expository rather than fundamental, especially if we interpret Keynes, with the Lange amendments, as not necessarily denying the influence of interest on the propensity to consume (time preference). The choice should be made to depend on convenience rather than on views concerning the factors properly belonging in a realistic framework. However, I do not see how a case can be made for the convenience of the liquidity-preference theory, or some analytical extension of it, if the discussion is concerned with the *structure* of interest rates.

If the Keynesian interest theory is interpreted as placing the emphasis on the assumed infinite elasticity of the liquidity function *at some far-above zero level of the interest-rate*, then the difference between Keynesian and Robertsonian views becomes somewhat more important. This, however, mainly reflects the fact that a break – or lack of continuity in the doctrinal development – does develop if stagnation is considered the essential content of the Keynesian theory. The significance of the Keynesian interest-floor proposition is that of explaining why the interest-rate does not adjust downward when, to restore full employment, it *should*. The Keynesian liquidity trap could of course be equally well expressed in terms of the loanable funds approach. In this approach the demand for idle balances must be treated as a constituent of the demand for funds or as a deduction from the supply. This constituent of the demand, or this deduction from the supply, could become infinitely responsive to interest-changes at any level of the interest-rate. But the belief that this would happen at some far-above zero level is specifically Keynesian, and this belief has a bearing on the stagnation thesis.

I wonder whether even this difference is very significant. The stagnation thesis does not hinge on it. The views of economists agree on the potential existence of a 'liquidity trap' somewhere in the neighbourhood of the zero rate. No one will part with money at the zero rate (or even at a very low positive rate which just suffices to compensate him for the institutional costs and inconveniences of security transactions) provided that he can keep money free of cost, or at negligible cost. This is another way of saying that very near the zero rate the liquidity-preference function, or its equivalent in some alternative model, undoubtedly does become infinitely elastic. Neither Robertson nor other authors have disregarded this in pre-Keynesian days. The real problem in connection with the stagnation doctrine, therefore, is whether to entrepreneurs the outlook seems favourable enough to induce them to invest on a sufficient scale, given the terms on which money can be borrowed and lent. If the outlook is chronically deficient, stagnation is the result. Robertson saw clearly that this *could* develop even if 'the' interest-rate declined to the neighbourhood of the zero level. It is somewhat less unlikely to occur if the interest-rate (say, the rate on long-term governments) 'got stuck' somewhere around 2 per cent, but I believe that in such circumstances most of us would be unwilling to attribute more than a small share of the responsibility to the 2 per cent. If we wish to interpret the Keynesian theory as the point of departure for the stagnation doctrine, the emphasis should be placed on the possibility that the 'marginal efficiency' may be chronically low and inelastic and that this may not be accompanied by a reduction of the propensity to save out of income. The emphasis should not, I think, be placed on the Keynesian interest theory.[5]

In the Robertsonian theory the business outlook may be deficient enough to reduce the amount of investment to any extent and this need not reduce the propensity to save out of income. Stagnation is a possibility in this theory, and the possibility arises because investment may be insufficient to fill the savings gap at the full-employment level of income, in spite of the interest-rate adjustments that may take place in such circumstances. It is sometimes suggested that this interpretation of stagnant constellations is specifically Keynesian because it pre-supposes the concept of the 'consumption function' – in the sense of $C = C\ (Y)$ – and this function made its first appearance in the *General Theory*. However, what is truly required for this sort of theory is not a *unique* relationship between consumption and income (which surely does not exist in reality) but recognition of the fact that *consumption and savings depend importantly on the level of income*, and that the further variables on which the savings-ratio may depend are not in all circumstances capable of assuming values which, at the given income-level, will equate investment to savings. In the Robertsonian analysis this is not only clearly recognised and explicitly discussed, but even emphasized. Conditions may exist under which the rate of interest would have to become negative to equate investment to saving, at a given level of the disposable income. We shall see later that in the Robertsonian approach compensatory monetary and fiscal policy are viewed as significant instruments for reducing 'inappropriate' fluctua-tions in income and employment, but they are incapable of establishing a negative money rate of interest. The treatment of this problem in Robertson's work of the nineteen-twenties does not of course suggest that a chronic condition of stagnation is to be anticipated. But Robert-sonian analysis does suggest that in depressions the shape of the rel-evant functions may very well be such that the equating of saving with private investment at the full-employment level would require a neg-ative money rate of interest which is not in reality obtainable.

The Robertsonian discussion of depressions leads to the conclusion that, if *we are faced with such conditions, public expenditure is the only effective means of compensatory policy*. One of the two chapters which were added to *Money* in 1947 takes account of the post-Keynesian literature on *secular* stagnation. The author does not feel that he can *refute* the prediction of pessimists that 'this time the wolf of stagnation is . . . ready to start gnawing at our vitals as soon as the processes of post-war reconstruction are complete'. Yet we are reminded that 'such prophecies have been made before and have not in fact been fulfilled, Dame Nature or Dame History having always in the end turned out to be keeping another card up her sleeve, though she has been sometimes rather slow in shaking it down'. The Robertsonian structure does possess a stagnationist corner, and some of his prescriptions for proper behaviour *in the corner* are in the nature of 'Keynesian' prescriptions (although they are chronologically pre-Keynesian). But the reader is not made to believe that he probably will be sitting in that corner during most of his life – war or no war. Outside that corner the long-run behaviour of interest-rates is dominated by investment opportunities which give rise to a demand for loanable funds, and by savings which are supplemented by money creation to supply these funds.[6]

ROBERTSONIAN ECONOMICS AND THE DISTINCTIVE FEATURES OF THE KEYNESIAN APPROACH

Does then Keynes minus stagnation amount to a more systematic presentation of Robertsonian (or perhaps Neo-Wicksellian) equilibrium: to a presentation which is more elegantly formalized, except that the equilibrium is taken out of the context of a continuous process and hence must be placed back in that context with tools not contained in the original Keynesian apparatus?

In the first and crudest approximation, Keynes minus stagnation does perhaps amount to this. But exclusive concern with overlapping elements would be misleading. The Keynesian theory possesses important features which distinguish it from the theories out of which it grew. It may be possible to argue that *all* these are connected with a stagnationist outlook, but in some cases the connection is sufficiently indirect to deserve attention under a separate heading. In the subsequent sections we shall return to distinctive features of the Robertsonian system.

The link between changes in income (below the full-employment level) and changes in employment is brought out more forcefully in the *General Theory* than in the earlier treatments. The method by which this is accomplished – measurement of output in wage units rather than in money of constant general purchasing power – is crude but nevertheless focuses attention on the fact that unemployment is the most significant of the social menaces which are created by depressions. This, I think is not merely a subjective judgment of value. It is a judgment pertaining to the conditions of survival of given social and economic institutions. At the same time, these conditions of survival include also the avoidance of chronic inflationary pressure, and we shall see later that for the analysis of price-output interactions the Keynesian theory is much less suitable than the Robertsonian. Keynes had to pay a price for the direct link between the magnitudes of his analytical system and the level of employment. Owing to measurement in wage units, changes in Keynesian 'income' are intended to express changes in employment and thereby in the level of real activity. While it is recognised that the wage unit itself (i.e., the deflator) *may* change when money expenditures do, the system is certainly not built for an analysis of changes in the deflator. The concept of aggregate physical output – the value of output corrected for *price changes* – also has serious pitfalls. But by first counting in money, then linking money flows to prices, and finally focusing their attention on physical output, Robertson and others were much less apt to detract attention from finite supply-elasticities and from the significance of price tendencies.

A similar argument can be developed with respect to the Keynesian treatment of the difference between changes in the general level of money wages and wage changes in specific industries is brought out more forcefully in the *General Theory* than in the earlier literature. Here again, the assumptions of Keynes's analysis are comparatively simple: With minor qualifications the general price level is assumed to move in the same proportion as the general wage level, and thus real wages are assumed to stay unaffected.[7] This may rest on the sweeping notion that it is not too unrealistic to represent the product markets as purely competitive, with labour playing the role of the only ultimate factor of production. However, in reality product markets are not purely competitive and it is not clear why all other income rates should change in the same proportion in which money wage rates do. In fact the *minimum* requirement for unchanging real wages rates (in the event of a general change in money wage rates) may be milder than was just suggested. The minimum requirement, it seems to me, is that monetary investment demand as well as consumer demand should change in the same proportion as the money wage rate and hence that the *ratio* of the demand for investment goods *to* the forthcoming consumer demand should be a parameter which is uninfluenced by the money-wage level. A change in the real wage rate would have to bring a change in this ratio (in equilibrium) because the propensity to consume would have to change. But in whatever fashion we wish to state the underlying assumptions they are certainly over-simplified, and it would be unreasonable to expect proportionate adjustment of effective demand and of prices to all changes in the general level of money wage rates, even aside from the Keynesian qualification pertaining to repercussions via liquidity and the rate of interest. At present we possess no general theory that would lead to definite conclusions concerning the size of the price movement which develops from a given movement in money wage-rates. But effective demand and prices do move when the general level of money wages changes and hence the framework suitable for the analysis of general wage changes must be different from that traditionally employed for the discussion of changes in small sectors of the economy. It would be quite wrong to believe that this was overlooked in the earlier literature in general, or in the Robertsonian analysis in particular. But it is true of Keynes more than of his predecessors that he devised a comprehensive technical apparatus which compels its user strictly to distinguish from the outset a general wage change from a specific. At the same time, it is true of Keynes in contrast to his predecessors that his simplifying assumptions reduce the problem of general wage changes to almost complete insignificance.

As compared to analysis of the Robertsonian type, Keynes's assumptions increase the usefulness of the Keynesian theory in some respects and reduce it in others. Such a statement could be defended in regard to the specifically Keynesian features so far considered and also in regard to the Kahn-Keynes multiplier relationship which probably had more influence on the analytic thinking of recent decades than any other 'Keynesian' innovation of the technical apparatus. The logical validity of the multiplier does not depend on the assumption that primary expenditure propagates itself exclusively via *consumption* responding but, whenever the channels of propagation become more complicated, the Kahn-Keynes multiplier approach must be supplemented by the analysis of these other channels. Only on severely restrictive assumptions can the supplementary analysis be placed into a reformulated multiplier framework, or into a framework derived exclusively from the Kahn-Keynes multiplier and the acceleration principle.

The Keynesian system as a whole is particularly well-built for the analysis of conditions influenced by a deflationary basic tendency; the wage unit of measurement is particularly well chosen for an economy with rigid money wages or with price-wage ratios which are unaffected by the money-wage level; the consumption function and the multiplier are particularly well constructed for conditions where savings out of income depend practically only on the income-level itself and where additional income, if not consumed, tends to be hoarded. The system strikes one as particularly rich if conditions of this sort are faced. But it will stand a good deal of amending and adapting. It is true of a substantial range of problems that the apparatus best suited for their understanding contains significant Keynesian additions, even though earlier savings-investment analysis, such as the Robertsonian, contained most of the basic ingredients required. It also contained significant elements with which Keynesians have almost completely dispensed, and which will gradually have to be collected again.

KEYNESIANISM, ROBERTSONIANISM AND THE QUESTION OF SOCIAL POLICY

The controversies of the early post *General Theory* years left many conservatives with the impression that Keynesianism is related to a political orientation which is of left-wing character, not in the sense of Marxism but in that of pronounced welfare-statism, or perhaps British Labour Party socialism. There has been considerably less temptation to associate Robertsonian economics with political creeds, but Robertson's choice and treatment of problems show a vivid interest in methods of making a market economy, such as is based on free choice, work efficiently. Is it then reasonable to interpret Keynesian economics as a body of doctrines which in some sense lies 'to the left of' Robertsonian economics?

I believe that the answer which this question deserves is a somewhat qualified 'no'. There exists only a very tenuous link between Keynesianism and a political programme of direct controls and (or) or large-scale social services financed by highly-graduated taxation. A Keynesian who opposes such a programme is not at all inconsistent. A

Keynesian who feels that he bases his support of such a programme on the *General Theory* is reading between lines, or at best is placing more emphasis on certain specific statements in the book than on others. Keynes too was vividly interested in making a market economy, such as is based on free choice, work efficiently.

It is true, however, that Keynes made it rather easy for a person to read between the lines and then to establish a link between his analysis and (non-Marxian) left-wing views. He did so mainly by showing no awareness of a problem which might have caught his eye. 'Errors of omission' in such a subtle sense of the term are not capable of being interpreted in any clear-cut way.

Keynes explained how in his opinion full employment could be accomplished. He showed no awareness of the fact that a consistent full-employment programme of his variety would result in substantial inflationary pressure, and would therefore in practice have to be supplemented by comprehensive direct controls. This would be true even if we could disregard the possibility that, in consequence of a shortage of cooperating factors, supply-elasticities may fall significantly before full employment is reached. Against the background of what might in effect become a full-employment guarantee, groups of workers and of employers would undoubtedly attempt to improve their relative position, as compared to other groups of the same sort, by pressing for higher rates of money income; and, given the guarantee in question, they would be capable of putting a wage-price escalator in motion throughout the economic system. There of course does exist a degree of integration (centralization) of economic activities which would reduce the number of groups with wills of their own to such an extent that they could 'collude' to prevent a self-defeating inflationary process. But extreme integration of this sort would by its very nature be a socialistic phenomenon; and in the absence of such integration, that is, on more realistic assumptions, comprehensive direct controls would be required, which are incompatible *per se* with the principles of a market economy based on free choice. Furthermore, by taking for granted a comprehensive system of controls and, for the greater part of the time, also the necessity of significant compensatory public expenditures, we would create a great deal of additional space for an ambitious programme of direct social services. In this kind of reasoning it is usually assumed that democratic political institutions are suitable for efficient administration of permanent direct controls: a very questionable assumption, which however need not detain us here. We merely mean to indicate in what way it is possible to construct a highway from Keynesian analysis to certain varieties of socialism. In building it, the constructors may make use also of Keynes's inclination to emphasize the consumption-raising effect of increased tax-graduation *more* than its possible adverse effect on the marginal efficiency schedule.

Yet it must be emphasized that Keynes himself did not build this highway. He did not say what in his opinion the proper policy would be if under a consistent full-employment programme a chronic inflationary pressure should develop. Consequently, it is possible also to construct a bridge from Keynesian analysis to policies of a very different sort which are geared to the wage-price level as well as to the level of employment. These policies can be bridged with Robertsonian analysis, just as easily as with the Keynesian. Compensatory employment policies can be used in a measure not exceeding that which is compatible with a reasonably stable (not necessarily constant) price level, *in the absence of direct controls.*

To say that Keynes *advocated* a policy of this sort would be no less arbitrary than to say that he built a highway to socialism (although he must have been more nearly a 'conservative' than a 'radical' Keynesian). The truth of the matter is that the Keynesian theory stops short of this dilemma. It has an empty spot in the area where the dilemma is located. In contrast, Robertsonian theory has no empty spot in this area. Robertson has consistently given a great deal of attention to the problem of interactions between movements in output and in prices. The reader may of course accept the result of Robertsonian analysis, and then, if he so wishes, may introduce the judgment of value that freedom from direct controls is less important than the avoidance of those fluctuations in employment which could not be eliminated without creating a chronic condition of suppressed inflation. But if he wishes to make this judgment, he cannot claim that he is moving in a vacant area of Robertsonian theory which must necessarily be filled either in this or in some other fashion. In the *General Theory* Keynes was primarily – almost exclusively – interested in employment. Robertson has been equally interested in price tendencies, and of course in trends in productivity.

This is an important difference. But crude political terminology is inadequate for expressing it.

THE UNEXPLOITED RESIDUE

To the forward-looking reader, the study of Robertson's work is interesting mainly because the 'Keynesian' late nineteen-thirties and nineteen-forties failed to assimilate essential ingredients of a reasonably complete theory of money and employment. Temporary lopsidedness lies in the nature of progress. But it had better remain temporary.

Robertsonian thinking is permeated by awareness of *structural* problems, that is, of the influence of the *composition* of aggregates on the size of these aggregates. Keynesianism of the late nineteen-thirties and of the 'forties suffers from lack of such awareness. Robertson's distinction between appropriate and inappropriate fluctuations of output is essentially a structural distinction in this sense. In the Robertsonian theory, alterations in the real operating costs of an industrial group, as well as alterations in the intensity of the relative demands of industrial groups for each others' products, require structural adjustments. Inventions are the most important reasons for changes in the real operating costs of an industry; in the *Study*, much more than in the later works, changing harvests are also given a prominent place. The structural or compositional adjustments in question are associated with changes in aggregate output which depend on demand and supply-elasticities. They play a significant role in the Robertsonian theory.

Cost reduction in a specific sector of the economy, and the reduction of the sector's selling price *relatively to the price charged by another sector*, may increase or decrease the output of the other sector. Fundamentally, with the money-veil lifted, the answer depends on the elasticity of demand of the other sector, *in terms of effort* (hence of output), for the products of the first sector. If, for example, this elasticity exceeds unity, the output of the other sector will rise. In a monetary economy – in contrast to a barter economy – these elasticities must be put together, so to speak, from price and income elasticities of *monetary* demand and supply, and hence they are influenced by monetary and fiscal policy. This amounts to saying that the observable elasticities of demand in terms of effort and the corresponding movements in aggregate output depend on monetary-fiscal policy as well as on the basic propensities of the public. What elasticities in terms of effort and hence what movements in output deserve to be favoured by policy?

'Appropriate' movements of output are movements (initial changes in specific sectors plus adjustments in others) which do not have to become reversed, that is, do not shoot beyond the mark. The elasticities of demand in terms of effort which underlie these movements are no different in the long run from what they are in the short run. Even a policy which wanted to limit itself to facilitating appropriate movements in aggregate output would not necessarily want to keep the general or average price level precisely constant. This is because changing relative prices with a constant general price level mean falling prices in specific sectors, and significant price reductions in important sectors are apt to impede the adjustments in the various sectors to the initial change. A mildly rising general price level is therefore more likely to have the effect of facilitating the 'appropriate' movements of output.

However, it would be unreasonable to try to suppress all 'inappropriate' fluctuations of output. The inappropriate movements in specific sectors are movements based on elasticities of demand in terms of effort, such as are different in the long run from what they are in the short run, and hence do result in a subsequent reversal (do carry the original adjustment to specific changes *beyond the mark*). They are consequences of essential characteristics of the economic system which on a sufficiently simplified level of analysis would appear as 'imperfections'. For example, indivisibilities of real capital force producers to invest either too much or too little, as compared with real requirements. If they invest too much, then this will lead to a subsequent sharp reduction of their demand for factors of production. The durability of plant and equipment has the same effect, since it may be viewed as indivisibility in the time-dimension. This is made clear by the kind of reasoning which is usually presented for explaining the acceleration principle. Also, individual producers are incompletely informed concerning the simultaneous expansionary and contractionary moves of other producers and they cannot dependably judge the consequences of their simultaneous actions. The length of the gestation periods to which certain investments are subject, aggravates these disturbances: by the time the investments become completed the conditions which called them forth may have changed considerably. The movements resulting from these factors are 'inappropriate' in the sense of carrying the original adjustments beyond the level which is appropriate in the long run. But only in a theoretical model could they be kept strictly apart from the appropriate movements. In the real world we must make up our minds as to the desirability of a whole complex of responses to initial changes, and such a complex always contains appropriate as well as inappropriate elements. Policy cannot be directed towards appropriate changes alone. But it can be directed toward the maximum amount of appropriate change (adjustment to technological improvement, to other real-cost changes, and to buyers' preferences) which is compatible with *not too much* inappropriate fluctuation. This proposition can of course not be formulated with the rigour of a mathematical theorem, because its interpretation depends on subjective weighing in individual instances. But it can serve as an eminently reasonable guiding principle.

The downturn is a direct consequence of saturation in the specific areas of investment in which inappropriate expansion has carried the adjustment beyond the mark. Frequently (but not always) the downturn is a consequence also of limits to the amount of investible funds which the monetary authority can let the banking system provide without producing an excessive degree of forced saving[8] by means of inflation. It seems to me that the second of these two causes, which may of course interact with the first,[9] is placed more into the forefront in *Banking Policy* than in the *Study* or in the later *Essays*. Hence those sections of *Banking Policy* which are specifically concerned with the downturn move pretty much along the lines of the 'monetary overinvestment theories', while the earlier and the later accounts distribute the emphasis more evenly, or even place other factors (saturation at a given level of technological knowledge) in the forefront. But what is placed in the forefront is invariably a structural aspect of dynamic development, rather than purely aggregative relationships.

The range of problems on which this analysis focuses attention has received little attention during the nineteen-thirties and 'forties. However, for some time there has existed renewed interest in certain elements of this complex. It consists of problems pertaining to the structure of output and to the structure of demands in a world where, as a consequence of uncertainty, producers must rely on guesswork; to the rate of technological advance; to production lags and, generally speaking, to timing in view of durability in indivisibility; and to the price tendencies most suitable for attaining the maximum degree of long-run progress without too much instability. No reader of Robertson can overlook the fact that these are problems of vital significance.

Concern with problems of the price level is likely also to revive interest in a proper synthesis of savings-investment analysis with ideas rooted in the quantity theory. Robertson's work shows clearly that such a synthesis existed in pre-Keynesian days. That equilibrium, or monetary expansion and contraction, can be expressed in terms of the relationship between savings and investment is neither more nor less true than that these conditions can be described with reference to the stock and the velocity of money. Neither the consumption function nor velocity (or any function from which alternative velocity values could be read) is truly stable, certainly not in the sense in which projections imply stability. It would be unreasonable to disregard the supply of money in the analysis of the factors which may produce changes in the income-consumption relation; and it would be unreasonable to disregard the propensity to consume in a search for factors which may bring about changes in velocity or in the quantity of money. Robertson saw this over sixty years ago. In this, as in some other respects, contemporary economists are on the way to a rediscovery.

But, on the whole, a series of rediscoveries is not what is needed. In the past decades a great deal has been built on foundations which were laid in the preceding era. While much of this will prove durable, there is much that will not. What will replace the temporary structures? What else can be built on the same or on similar foundations?

NOTES

1. The writer of this article expresses his thanks to Professors Norman S. Buchanan, Howard S. Ellis and Lloyd G. Reynolds for valuable suggestions.

2. The first by the London School of Economics in 1948; the second by Nisbet and Co, London, at the Cambridge University Press, in the Hand-

books series now under the editorship of Mr C. W. Guillebaud; the third by Augustus M. Kelley (New York) and Staples Press (London) in 1949.

3.   M. Labordère was not a professional economist. He seems to have impressed both Professor Robertson and Lord Keynes with his insight and imagination. (Robertson tells us of Labordère, that 'he lived in Paris and that he owned some small farms in the Jura. . . . By the time I knew him he was a very strange but very likeable old man, rather deaf and with a long white beard, much absorbed in a religion strangely compounded of Buddhism and Islam'.) The article in question was originally published in the *Revue de Paris* in 1908 and it presented in allegoric form an 'overinvestment' interpretation of the American crisis of 1907, making it clear that the basic structure of such an argument can be expressed in non-monetary terms, and moving from there to the monetary level. Two sentences which are characteristic of the views expressed in the article: '*la crise est venue parce qu' on a voulu faire trop vite trop de chose à la fois'*, and '*nous plaçons nos èconomies avant de les avoir faites'*.

4.   Such as, for example, 'Saving and Hoarding', reprinted from the 1933 volume of *The Economic Journal*; 'Industrial Fluctuation and the Rate of Interest', from the 1934 volume of *The Manchester School* (reprinted also in American Economic Association, *Readings in Business Cycle Theory* (Philadelphia: Blakiston Co. 1944); 'Mr Keynes and Finance', from the 1938 volume of *The Economic Journal* (reprinted also in American Economic Association, *Readings in the Theory of Income Distribution* (Philadelphia: Blakiston Co., 1946)).

5.   The worsening of business expectations (adverse shift of the marginal efficiency function) cannot lead to underemployment if the liquidity function has zero elasticity throughout the range of interest-rates actually ruling *and* does *not* shift to the right; and whatever underemployment does to develop when the liquidity function is not vertical throughout the relevant range, or when it does shift to the right, can be remedied by increasing the supply of money in wage units except if the liquidity function is *infinitely* elastic at the ruling interest-rate and at the same time the consumption function fails to shift upward with a rise in the real value of cash balances. Therefore chronic stagnation, such as is not simply a matter of insufficient money supply in wage units, does assume that business expectations are sufficiently unfavourable to lower the interest-rate to a floor level at which the liquidity function is infinitely elastic. But if expectations are sufficiently unfavourable, then it does not matter whether the floor level lies at 2 per cent or at 0.1 per cent. The proposition that a floor level would be hit before the rate becomes negative is, and has been, entirely uncontroversial. Allowance for the institutional costs of lending and borrowing obviously leads to the conclusion that the floor must lie above zero.

6. In Keynesian terminology investment opportunities tend to raise the rate of interest because they create a demand for money ('finance'). The activity which Robertson defines as saving (p. 269, supra) tends to reduce the rate of interest because it reduces the amount of money *needed* under the Keynesian income motive (for consumption), and hence increase the amount of money *available* for finance and for speculative purposes.

7. The Keynesian qualification that general money wage changes are associated with a change in the existing degree of liquidity in terms of wage units (and hence with a change in the interest-rate and in investment, and via the multiplier also in consumption) is perhaps not 'minor' from an analytical point of view. The significance of the qualification becomes small if the liquidity function is assumed to be very elastic; and its significance is generally small for the appraisal of Keynesian views as a whole (in contrast to the appraisal of the formal apparatus itself) because in connection with this qualification Keynes places the main emphasis on the fact that it would always be possible to adjust the supply money directly. Any favourable effect of a general wage change could be obtained in a much simpler way by this direct method, and any unfavourable effect could be offset by the use of this method. The theory assumes that a general change in money wage rates affects aggregate output merely via liquidity and interest (aside from qualifications which are *really* minor). I believe that a general change in money wage rates is likely to have an effect also on the 'marginal efficiency', that is to say, I see no good reason for assuming that, aside from repercussion via the interest-rate, the monetary demand for investment goods tends to adjust in the same proportion as the demand for consumer goods.

8. Forced saving (automatic lacking) in the sense of the diversion of goods *from* their producers (i.e., *from* recipients of money incomes already earned) *to* investors who are borrowing 'new money' from the banking system.

9. 'Saturation' is not an absolute concept. An area of investment activity may be 'saturated' at high rates of interest and not 'saturated' under an easy money policy.

Index